The Jane Austen Marriage Manual

The Jane Austen Marriage Manual

HELEN AMY

AMBERLEY

First published 2017
This edition first published 2017

Amberley Publishing
The Hill, Stroud
Gloucestershire, GL5 4EP

www.amberley-books.com

Copyright © Helen Amy 2017

The right of Helen Amy to be identified as the Author
of this work has been asserted in accordance with the
Copyrights, Designs and Patents Act 1988.

All rights reserved. No part of this book may be reprinted
or reproduced or utilised in any form or by any electronic,
mechanical or other means, now known or hereafter invented,
including photocopying and recording, or in any information
storage or retrieval system, without the permission in writing
from the Publishers.

British Library Cataloguing in Publication Data.
A catalogue record for this book is available from the British Library.

ISBN 978 1 4456 5172 9 (paperback)
ISBN 978 1 4456 5173 6 (ebook)

Typeset in 11pt on 13.5pt Sabon.
Typesetting and Origination by Amberley Publishing.
Printed in the UK.

Contents

Willoughby was a young man of good abilities, quick imagination, lively spirits, and open, affectionate manners. He was exactly formed to engage Marianne's heart; for with all this, he joined not only a captivating person, but a natural ardour of mind which was now roused and increased by the example of her own, and which recommended him to her affection beyond everything else. His society became gradually her most exquisite enjoyment. They read, they talked, they sang together; his musical talents were considerable; and he read with all the sensibility and spirit which Edward had unfortunately wanted.

Introduction

Jane Austen was born and brought up in rural England in the late Georgian period. The society she lived in, and wrote about, was a patriarchal one, in which most women were dependent, second-class citizens.

Patriarchy was founded on the biblical precept that woman was the 'helpmeet' of man, as Eve was to Adam. The Bible decreed that women were subservient to men and their role was to support and obey them. The natural God-given characteristics of the sexes were considered to fit them for their respective positions. Men's intelligence, rationality and judgement fitted them for power and control. Thus men ran public life, business and politics in the eighteenth century, while women's 'softer' qualities, such as compliance, gentleness and devotion, equipped them for their roles as wife, mother and housekeeper.

The institution of marriage was very important in Georgian and Regency England. Not only was it the foundation of a strong and stable society, but it also protected the ownership of land and helped to preserve ancestral homes for future generations.

Women of the middle and upper classes were under great pressure to marry. Marriage was the only way for them to fulfil their God-given destiny as wives and mothers, and girls were prepared for their future roles in the domestic sphere from an early age.

Married women were accorded a higher status in society than single women. Spinsters were reviled as unnatural social failures who were deemed to have brought shame on their families by not fulfilling the roles intended for them by God. There was a widespread belief that even a bad marriage was better than no marriage at all.

Women's financial dependence on men added to the pressure to find a husband. They were excluded by law from nearly all professions and from holding public office. It was not considered appropriate for women of the respectable classes to work unless forced to by dire necessity, and for those who had to work there were very few opportunities available. It was also difficult for women to inherit money and property due to the custom of primogeniture. Furthermore, marriage, for most women, was the only way to gain independence from their parents and acquire a home or 'establishment' of their own, even though they were merely exchanging dependence on one man for dependence on another. For these reasons marriage was the only real ambition for the majority of women of the better-off classes.

As the eighteenth century progressed there were fewer arranged marriages and a trend was growing towards marrying for love. This was due to an increasing realization that love was necessary for a happy marriage. Mercenary motives still played a part, however. Women needed to marry well because they acquired their status from, and were defined by, the men responsible for them, and they needed to find a husband who could support them and provide a good home. Most marriages were, therefore, a combination of a love match and a financial arrangement.

Conduct and Advice Literature

Life in the polite society of Georgian and Regency England was governed by rules of etiquette and codes of acceptable behaviour. These were set out in conduct and advice literature – a popular literary genre aimed at educating people in social norms. There was a rapidly growing readership for all types of such literature but particularly that aimed at women, for whom much more was written than for men.

The purpose of much of this literature was to educate females of the better-off classes about their subservient place in society, and their roles and duties in life. It was also intended to reinforce the female characteristics admired by men such as chastity, modesty, passivity and obedience.

Included in this conduct and advice literature was guidance on the detailed protocol and complex rules that had to be observed, by both sexes, during courtship. Knowing and keeping these rules was essential, as there were severe consequences for breaking them, especially for women.

This book follows the various stages that a young lady in Jane Austen's England passed through, from 'coming out' into society to her wedding day and beyond. The text is accompanied by a selection of advice and guidance taken from late seventeenth-, eighteenth- and early nineteenth-century manuals, treatises, essays and letters. Material is also taken from women's magazines and the novels of Jane Austen, which are often described as 'courtship novels'. These novels are love stories which end in happy marriages after the heroines have negotiated the potential pitfalls of courtship and learned important lessons before winning the man they love. Like the advice literature, Austen's novels provide a fascinating insight into courtship and marriage during her lifetime, and also reveal her views on these important matters.

The unusual punctuations and spellings in the primary source texts have not been drawn to the reader's attention as they are too numerous. (For notes on the sources used and their authors see page XX.)

PART ONE

COURTSHIP

Coming Out and Finding a Suitable Man

A young lady had to go through a number of stages before she acquired a husband. The first of these was 'coming out' into society at the age of sixteen and entering the marriage market. There were certain signs which indicated whether a girl was 'out' or 'not out'. Before she came out a girl was always accompanied by a chaperone, she was quiet and reserved in company and she wore a demure 'close bonnet' with a deep brim when she was outdoors. A girl could not come out before her older sister.

Men were not supposed to show any interest in a girl who was not yet out. In *Mansfield Park* Tom Bertram describes the difficulties this sometimes caused:

… we went after them, and found them on the pier, – Mrs. and the two Miss Sneyds, with others of their acquaintance. I made my bow in form; and as Mrs. Sneyd was surrounded by men, attached myself to one of her daughters, walked by her side all the way home, and made myself as agreeable as I could,- the young lady perfectly easy in her manners, and as ready to talk as to listen. I had not a suspicion that I could be doing anything wrong. They looked just the same: both well-dressed, with veils and parasols like other girls; but I afterwards found that I had been giving all my attention to the youngest, who was not out, and had most excessively offended the eldest. Miss Augusta ought not to have been noticed for the next six months; and Miss Sneyd, I believe, has never forgiven me.

The age for coming out was so young because women married at a young age – the average age was just over twenty-two years. Upper-class girls came out after being presented at Court during the London Season and middle-class girls came out at a formal ball, either a private one or a public one at the local assembly rooms.

Once out, a girl was chaperoned by an older or a married woman in public places and public carriages. There were several other important rules which had to be observed in order to protect a girl's reputation. The strictest decorum had to be maintained in the company of men; a girl should never be alone with a man; and it was not permitted for a girl to dance more than two dances with the same man in one evening, or it could be assumed that they had 'reached an agreement', or, in other words, that they were engaged. When a girl was out she was expected to behave with confidence in society and she was allowed to join in conversations. It was acceptable for girls who were out to walk about in groups, as the Bennet sisters do in *Pride and Prejudice,* or in pairs.

Mothers had the important task of taking their daughters to places where they could meet suitable men of their own class. In *Mansfield Park,* Lady Bertram, who is a lazy and neglectful mother, fails to fulfil this duty to her daughters. They are left to the malign influence of her sister, Mrs Norris, who encourages the ill-fated match between Maria Bertram and Mr Rushworth.

A young lady had to be careful not to make it obvious that she was seeking a husband, as it was up to the man to do the wooing and winning. Men judged a woman's suitability as a potential wife on her appearance, behaviour, manners, accomplishments and wealth.

Responding to Attention and Getting to Know Each Other

After coming out and entering the marriage market, a young lady had to be ready to receive attention from potential suitors. As at every stage in the process of finding a husband, there were important rules to observe. A woman could only respond to attention from a man, she could not make a move herself. When a man showed an interest in a woman, she had to behave as if she had not noticed. This is why Jane Bennet in *Pride and Prejudice* is careful not to show her awareness of Mr Bingley's obvious attraction to her.

Although a woman was not permitted to express her interest in a man, this rule could be circumvented by using a friend or a brother as a go-between to drop hints. Breaking the rules in this way was risky, however, because of the scandal caused if a woman was caught breaking the rules.

Once a courtship started there were more, and stricter, rules to follow. These were designed to protect a woman's reputation and to protect a man from being ensnared against his will. A woman's virginity was regarded as her greatest asset and this could be called into question if she behaved incorrectly.

The rules which governed courtship made it difficult for a young couple to get to know each other, especially the requirement that the woman was chaperoned at all times. The couple were not allowed to be left alone together in a room, to travel alone together or to converse privately. They could not address each other by their Christian names, exchange presents or correspond with one another, and they could only dance two dances together in one evening. Kissing was forbidden, as was touching, except briefly with gloved hands while dancing and walking to and from a dance. A couple could only bow or curtsey when acknowledging each other or when saying hello and goodbye.

Courtships were conducted in public and any deviation from the code of conduct was soon noticed. If her reputation was lost a woman would be punished by social ostracism and her family's reputation could also be tainted. Sometimes a woman was forced to marry a man against her will because she had, for example, appeared to be too familiar or too affectionate towards him.

Jane Austen herself took the risk of breaking the rules in 1796 during a brief, youthful flirtation with

But, indeed, Elinor, it is Marianne's. I am almost sure it is, for I saw him cut it off. Last night, after tea, when you and Mamma went out of the room, they were whispering and talking together as fast as could be, and he seemed to be begging something of her, and presently he took up her scissors and cut off a long lock of her hair, for it was all tumbled down her back; and he kissed it, and folded it up in a piece of white paper, and put it into his pocket-book."

a young man named Tom Lefroy. Jane and Tom, the nephew of the rector of Ashe in Hampshire, got to know each other at a number of social events when he stayed with his uncle over the Christmas period. A mutual affection developed and Jane became aware that she was exposing herself to gossip by dancing and sitting down with Tom too much. Jane's sister Cassandra scolded her for not behaving with the utmost propriety.

In *Sense and Sensibility* the impetuous Marianne Dashwood breaks a number of the rules of courtship in her relationship with Willoughby. Not only does she go out alone with Willoughby soon after meeting him, but she allows him to take a lock of her hair and sends him a letter. Her behaviour is so reckless that Marianne's sensible sister Elinor wrongly concludes that 'some kind of engagement had subsisted between Willoughby and Marianne'.

The Proposal

When a man was certain that his feelings were reciprocated by the woman he was courting he would make a proposal of marriage. Proposals took place in a private setting and were often the first time a couple were alone together. The most tender and romantic proposal of marriage in Jane Austen's novels, that of Mr Knightley to Emma, takes place in the secluded shrubbery walk in the garden at Hartfield.

Although a woman was not allowed to show interest in a man or make any moves to initiate a courtship, she had one important prerogative: the choice to accept or refuse a proposal. In *Northanger Abbey* Henry Tilney points this out when he says 'man has the advantage of choice, woman only the power of refusal'. Most proposals, which were usually made in person or by letter, were accepted as it was unlikely for a courtship to have progressed so far if a couple were not serious about each other. It was also considered bad form for a woman to encourage the attentions of a man she did not like. If an undesirable proposal was received, however, the correct response was to decline it with civility and sensitivity.

When considering a proposal there were a number of important factors for a woman to take into account. As well as the vital question of whether the man would make her happy, she had to bear in mind the man's position in society, as marrying beneath one's social class was frowned upon. A woman also had to consider her suitor's ability to support her and maintain a household as well as the likelihood of her parents approving of the match. She also had to be aware of whether there was any mercenary motive behind a man's proposal, as some men married for financial reasons. A good example of this occurs in *Sense and Sensibility*, when Willoughby rejects Marianne Dashwood in favour of the wealthy Miss Grey, so that he can pay off his debts.

Accepting a proposal of marriage was a very serious step, as the difficulties and expense of divorce made it almost impossible to end an unhappy one. The vast majority of those who made a bad choice had to live with it, as Mr Bennet does in *Pride and Prejudice*. Mr Bennet had been captivated by his wife's youth and beauty and 'that appearance of good-humour which youth and beauty generally give'. It was not long, however, before her 'weak understanding and illiberal mind' put an end to her husband's affection and respect for her. Mr Bennet sought consolation for his unhappiness in the countryside and books.

Once a woman accepted a proposal the next step was for the man to seek the consent of her father, or male guardian, before an engagement could be announced.

Surprise proposals were not unusual. Many women, including Jane Austen, received unexpected proposals of marriage. Jane's came from Harris Bigg-Wither, the brother of three of her friends, whom Jane did not know very well. She initially accepted this offer, but had second thoughts and soon withdrew her acceptance. Jane was briefly tempted by the material and other advantages that marriage to Bigg-Wither would have provided. However, she quickly realised that she could not marry a man she did not love.

In *Pride and Prejudice* Elizabeth Bennet receives two unexpected proposals of marriage and is completely taken aback by both of them. The first proposal comes from Mr Collins, who has been advised by his patroness, Lady Catherine de Bourgh, to find a wife, and has come to Longbourne with the intention of proposing to one of the Bennet sisters. Elizabeth indignantly rejects

Mr Collins' proposal. To add insult to injury, Elizabeth has to reject him five times before Mr Collins accepts that she is not refusing him merely because 'it is usual with young ladies to reject the addresses of the man whom they secretly mean to accept'.

The second offer of marriage comes from Mr Darcy, who has fallen in love with Elizabeth against his better judgement, and despite her family's lowly position and her mother's embarrassing behaviour. Elizabeth indignantly rejects this proposal as well – it is her goal to marry a man whom she loves and respects and who will make her happy. It is not until the end of the novel that Mr Darcy fulfils these criteria.

In *Mansfield Park* a surprise proposal occurs when Henry Crawford applies to Sir Thomas Bertram for permission to propose to his niece Fanny Price, much to Fanny's surprise and horror. Another unexpected proposal occurs in *Emma,* who is astonished and highly offended to receive an offer of marriage from Mr Elton, her social inferior. Emma is under the misapprehension that Mr Elton is in love with Harriet Smith when, in fact, she herself is the object of his affections.

By the late Georgian period there were fewer arranged marriages than earlier in the century because of the realisation of the importance of happiness in marriage. Women's financial dependence on men, however, led many to marry for financial reasons. Jane Austen's novels show the financial pressure women were under to marry and, preferably, to marry well. In *Pride and Prejudice* she describes marriage as 'the only honourable provision for well-educated young women of small fortune, and however uncertain of giving happiness, must be their pleasantest preservative from want'. Charlotte Lucas's motives for marrying Mr Collins show how some women had to make sacrifices to avoid spinsterhood and poverty. Charlotte tells Elizabeth that she has 'no romantic ideas about marriage based on love', and that she is prepared to put up with the irksome Mr Collins to get a home of her own and financial security. Elizabeth Bennet voices Jane Austen's own views on such marriages when she predicts that it will be impossible for Charlotte 'to be tolerably happy in the lot she has chosen'.

When Jane Austen's niece Fanny Knight sought her advice regarding a relationship with a man about whom she had ambivalent feelings, Jane responded by saying, 'Nothing can be compared to the misery of being bound without love, bound to one and preferring another.' Fanny decided to end the relationship and eventually found a man she loved enough to marry.

The Engagement, Marriage Settlement and Wedding Arrangements

Once a marriage proposal was accepted, and parental consent had been obtained, the engagement took place. The giving of a formal engagement or betrothal ring was unusual, but posy rings were often exchanged. Posy rings were inscribed on the inside with short sentimental verses, such as 'Providence divine hath made me thine' and 'None to me so dear as thee.' These rings were not meant to be a sign of a firm commitment. No rings are given or exchanged when engagements take place in Jane Austen's novels.

An engagement was regarded as a contract and, therefore, breaking one off was a very serious matter. A man over the age of twenty-one could not break off an engagement, but a woman could, although this would earn her the reputation of a jilt and lead to scandal and gossip. It could also affect her family's reputation.

Once a couple became engaged there was some relaxation in the rules governing their behaviour. They were permitted to use each other's Christian names in private and they could correspond, but in a restrained manner, without expression of excessive feelings.

Secret engagements were strongly disapproved of, but these sometimes occurred if families were unhappy about a match. However, as shown by the secret engagements of Frank Churchill and Jane Fairfax in *Emma* and of Edward Ferrars and Lucy Steele in *Sense and Sensibility*, they could lead to confusion, misunderstandings, subterfuge and deceit.

The next step, after the engagement, was the drawing up of the Marriage Settlement, which dealt with the financial aspects of the marriage. This was very important, as once a woman was married, her legal and financial rights were transferred from her father to her husband. The bride's parents were expected to provide a dowry; the bride was entitled to the interest on this sum during her lifetime and she could leave it to her children. Agreement was also reached on provision for the wife and children if the husband died.

Legal Requirements

The legal requirements for marriage were laid down in Hardwicke's Marriage Act of 1753. Under the terms of this Act, parental consent was required if either of the parties was under the age of twenty-one.

There were three different ways by which a couple could get married. The first option, which involved no cost, was by the reading of banns in the parish church of one of the couple. The banns were read, announcing the forthcoming marriage during three successive Sunday services. If no objections were raised to the marriage, it could take place within ninety days of the reading of the banns. The ceremony had to be held in a public chapel or church, be conducted by a member of the authorised clergy and be recorded in the marriage register, with the signature of the bride and groom, witnesses and the minister. The ceremony had to take place within the canonical hours of eight in the morning and twelve noon.

The second option was to skip the banns and marry by common or ordinary licence, which could be obtained from a local clergyman or from Doctors Commons in

London, at a cost of ten shillings. The ceremony had to be conducted within the canonical hours, in the parish in which one of the parties had resided for a minimum of fifteen days. It is by common licence that Wickham and Lydia Bennet marry in *Pride and Prejudice.* Their marriage ceremony takes place in St Clement's Church in London, as Wickham's lodgings are in that parish.

The most expensive way to get married was by a special licence, which was obtained from the Archbishop of Canterbury. This licence allowed a couple to marry wherever they wanted and at whatever hour they wished. Only the very wealthy could afford to marry by special licence as it cost between four and five pounds.

In *Pride and Prejudice,* on hearing that Elizabeth is to marry the wealthy Mr Darcy, Mrs Bennet excitedly exclaims 'And a special license. You must and shall be married by a special license.' It is not clear in the novel if Mrs Bennet gets her wish or the young couple marry in the local parish church.

For those under the age of twenty-one, without parental consent to get married, there was only one option: elopement to Gretna Green, just over the border in Scotland. Parental consent was not necessary in Scotland, where marriage laws were not as strict as in England. Elopement to Gretna Green required courage because it caused great scandal and damaged the reputation of the couple and their families. In *Pride and Prejudice,* when Lydia elopes with Wickham, her family fear that they are heading for Gretna Green and urgent attempts are made to find them before this happens. Fortunately, Mr Darcy locates them and pays Wickham to marry Lydia in a respectable wedding ceremony.

On the Mode of Introducing Young Women into General Society.
(*An Enquiry into the Duties of the Female Sex* – Thomas Gisborne, 1797)

When the business of education, whether conducted at home or at a public seminary, draws towards a conclusion, the next object that occupies the attention of the parent is what she terms the introduction of her daughter into the world. Emancipated from the shackles of instruction, the young woman is now to be brought forward to act her part on the public stage of life. And as though liberty were a gift unattended with temptations to inexperienced youth; as though vivacity, openness of heart, the consciousness of personal accomplishments and of personal beauty, would serve rather to counteract than to aggravate those temptations; the change of situation is not unfrequently heightened by every possible aid of contrast. Pains are taken, as it were, to contrive, that when the dazzled stranger shall step from the nursery and the lecture-room, she shall plunge at once into a flood of vanity and dissipation. Mewed up from every prying gaze, taught to believe that her first appearance is the subject of universal expectation, tutored to beware above all things of tarnishing the lustre of her attractions by "mauvaise bonte", stimulated with desire to outshine her equals in age and rank, she burns with impatience for the hour of displaying her perfections: till at length, intoxicated beforehand with anticipated flatteries, she is launched, in the pride of ornament, on some occasion of festivity; and from that time forward thinks by day and dreams by night of amusements, and of dress, and of compliments, and of admirers.

I believe this picture to convey no exaggerated representation of the state of things, which is often witnessed in the higher ranks of society. I fear, too, that it is a picture to which the practice of the middle ranks, though at present not fully corresponding, bears a continually increasing resemblance. The extreme, however, which has been described, has, like every other extreme, its opposite. There are mothers who profess to initiate their daughters, almost from the cradle, into what they call the knowledge of life; and pollute the years of childhood with an instilled attachment to the card-table; with habits of flippancy and pertness, denominated wit; with an "easiness" of manners, which ought to be named effrontery; and with a knowledge of tales of scandal unfit to be mentioned by anyone but in a court of justice. Both these extremes are most dangerous to every thing that is valuable in the female character; to every thing on which happiness in the present world and in a future world depends. But of the two the latter is the more pernicious. In that system war is carried on almost from infancy, and carried on in the most detestable manner, against female delicacy and innocence. In the former that delicacy and that innocence are exposed under the greatest disadvantages to the sudden influence of highly fascinating allurements. It may be hoped however, that, coming to the encounter as yet little impaired, they may have some chance of escaping without severe injury. At any rate, be this chance ever so small, it is greater than the probability, that when assailed from their earliest dawn by slow poison incessantly administered, they should ultimately survive.

To accustom the mind by degrees to the trials which it must learn to withstand, yet to shelter it from insidious temptations, while it is unable to discern and to shun the

26

snare, is the first rule which wisdom suggests with regard to all trials and temptations whatever. To this rule too much attention cannot be paid in the mode of introducing a young woman into the common habits of social intercourse. Let her not be distracted in the years by nature particularly designed for the cultivation of the understanding and the acquisition of knowledge, by the turbulence and glare of polite amusements. Let her not be suffered to taste the draught which the world offers to her, until she has learned that, if there be sweetness on the surface, there is venom deeper in the cup; until she has acquired a right judgment and a well-directed taste as to the pursuits and pleasures of life, or, according to the expression of the Apostle, has become disposed "to approve the things which are excellent;" and is fortified with those principles of temperance and rectitude, which may guard her against unsafe indulgence. Let vanity, and other unwarrantable springs of action, prompt, at all times, to exert their influence on the female character, and at no time likely to exert an influence more dangerous than when a young woman first steps into public life, be curtailed, as far as may be safely practicable, of the powerful assistance of novelty. Altogether to preclude that assistance is impossible. But it may be disarmed of much of its force by gradual familiarity. Let that gradual familiarity take place under the superintendence of parents and near relations, and of friends of approved sobriety and discretion. Let not the young woman be consigned to some fashionable instructress, who, professing at once to add the last polish to education, and to introduce the pupil into the best company, will probably dismiss her thirsting for admiration; inflamed with ambition; devoted to dress and amusements; initiated in the science and the habit of gaming; and prepared to deem every thing right and indispensable, which is or shall be recommended by modish example. Let her not be abandoned in her outset in life to the giddiness and mistaken kindness of fashionable acquaintance in the metropolis; nor forwarded under their convoy to public places, there to be whirled, far from maternal care and admonition, in the circles of levity and folly, into which, even had maternal care and admonition been at hand to protect her, she ought not to have been permitted to step. At this very important season, while the mother selects with cautious discrimination, and limits within narrow bounds both as to time and expence, the scenes of public resort and entertainment, to which her youthful charge is now to be suffered to have access; let her cultivate in the mind of the latter with augmented solicitude those principles, dispositions, and habits, which may lead her not only cheerfully to acquiesce in the course adopted, but even spontaneously and decidedly to prefer it to a system of less guarded indulgence. Let a double share of attention be exerted to preserve and strengthen in her breast a sense of the frailty of human nature; of the necessity of constantly looking up to divine support; of the transitory and inconsiderable worth of temporal things compared with eternity; of the superiority of the peaceful and heartfelt joys, which flow from the discharge of duty and the animating hopes of the favour of God, over every other gratification. All these principles are menaced, when fresh inlets of ensnaring pleasures are opened. Let parental vigilance and love gently point out to the daughter, on every convenient occasion, what is proper or improper in the conduct of the persons of her own age, with whom she is in any degree conversant, and also the grounds of the approbation or disapprobation expressed. Let parental counsel and authority be prudently exercised in regulating the choice of her associates. And at the same time that she is habituated to regard distinctions of wealth and rank, as circumstances wholly unconnected with personal worth; let her companions be in general neither much above her own level, nor much below it; lest she should be led to ape the opinions, the expensiveness, and the fashionable follies of persons in a station higher than her own; or, in her intercourse with those of humbler condition to assume airs of contemptuous and domineering superiority. Solicitude on the part of parents, to consult the welfare of their child in these points, will probably be attended with a further consequence of no small benefit to themselves; when it persuades them to an encreased degree of circumspection as to the visitors whom they encourage at home, and the society which they frequent abroad.

Considerations Antecedent to Marriage
(*An Enquiry into the Duties of the Female Sex* – Thomas Gisborne, 1797)

... The prospect of passing a single month with an acquaintance, whose society we know to be unpleasing, is a prospect from which every mind recoils. Were the time of intercourse antecedently fixed to extend to a year, or to a longer period, our repugnance would be proportionally great. Were the term to reach to the death of one of the parties, the evil would appear in foresight scarcely to be endured. But further; let it be supposed, not only that the parties were to be bound during their joint lives to the society of each other; but that their interests were to be inseparably blended together in all circumstances. And, in the next place, let it also be supposed that the two parties were not to engage in this association on terms of perfect equality; but that one of them was necessarily to be placed as to various particulars, in a state of subordination to the other. What caution would be requisite in each of the parties, what especial caution would be requisite in the party destined to subordination, antecedently to such an engagement! How diversified, how strict, how persevering should be the inquiries of each respecting the other, and especially of the latter respecting the former! Unless the dispositions, the tempers, the habits, the genuine character, and inmost principles were mutually known; what rational hope, what tolerable chance of happiness could subsist? And if happiness should not be the lot of the two associates, would not their disquietudes be proportionate to the closeness of their union? Let this reasoning be transferred to the case of marriage.

Whether marriage establishes between the husband and the wife a perfect equality of rights, or conveys to the former a certain degree of superiority over the latter, is a point not left among Christians to be decided by speculative arguments. The intimation of the divine will, communicated to the first woman immediately after the fall, is corroborated by various injunctions delivered in the New Testament. "Let the wife see that she reverence her husband."- "Wives, submit yourselves unto your own husbands as unto the Lord; for the husband is the head of the wife, even as Christ is the head of the church; – therefore as the church is subject unto Christ, so let the wives be to their own husbands in every thing." The command in the second of these passages is so explicit, and illustrated by a comparison so impressive, that it is needless to recite other texts of a similar import. The obedience, however, which is here enjoined by the Apostle, is not unlimited obedience. Were a husband presumptuously to require his wife to infringe the property or other rights of a third person, or to transgress any of the divine laws, she would be bound to obey God rather than man. And it is very possible that he might be in other respects so unreasonable and injurious in his injunctions, that she might with justice conceive herself exempted, as to those particular instances, from the obligation of implicit submission to his authority. St. Paul directs children to obey their parents, and servants their masters, "in **all** things." Yet it is manifest that his direction was not intended to reach to things sinful, nor perhaps to other extreme cases which might be devised. It is reasonable, therefore, and is it also conformable to the general mode of *conveying* moral directions which is adopted in the Scriptures, to understand his strong declaration concerning the authority of a husband as limited by restrictions and exceptions, corresponding to those with which his equally strong declarations concerning the authority of parents and of masters are manifestly to be understood. But though in cases such as have been supposed the duty of female obedience is suspended, it is suspended in these only. She who is commanded to "be subject to her head, the husband, as the church is subject to Christ, its head," cannot reasonably doubt that under all other circumstances faithful and willing obedience is a branch of her connubial duty.

A branch of duty in its nature so important and extensive, ought to be considered antecedently to marriage with religious scrupulousness. And while the obligation is acknowledged, let not the ends for which it is imposed be misconceived. Let not pride or ignorance be for a moment permitted to suggest that the Father of the universe, in allotting obedience to the wife, has displayed a partial regard to the welfare and comfort of the husband. Eternal wisdom, incapable of error and of caprice, has in this dispensation consulted her happiness no less than that of her associate. You admit that it was desirable to prevent or to lessen the bickerings, the conflicts, the pertinacious contrariety of plans and projects, which, in a state imperfect as human nature is, would perpetually arise and involve families in unceasing confusion, were each party free from any obligation to acquiesce in the decision of the other. By what method then, were we to consult the dictates of unbiased judgement, should we deem the object most likely to be attained? Undoubtedly by the method which Providence has adopted; by assigning to one of the partners in marriage a fixed pre-eminence over the other. If this point be once conceded, there cannot be room for much hesitation as to the only remaining question; to which of the two parties would it be wisest and best that the pre-eminence should be assigned? It is on man that the burden of the most laborious offices in life, of those offices which require the greatest exertions, the deepest reflection, and the most comprehensive judgement, is devolved. Man, that he may be qualified for the discharge of these offices, has been furnished by his Creator with powers of investigation and of foresight in a somewhat larger measure than the other sex, who have been recompensed by an ample share of mental endowments of a different kind. It seems therefore an appointment both reasonable in its nature, and most conducive to the happiness, not only of the man himself, but of his wife, of his children, and of all his connections, that he should be the person to whom the superiority should be committed. But Heaven has not left the wife destitute or neglected. Security is provided for her in various ways against an arbitrary and tyrannical exercise of power on the part of the husband. Some limitations to which his authority is subjected have already been noticed.

These, if he deserve the name of a Christian, he well knows. He knows too, that if he be entrusted with power, he acts under a proportionate responsibility, that he acts under the all seeing eye of his future Judge. And if the Scriptures are on the one hand express in enjoining obedience to the wife; they are no less explicit on the other in reminding the husband of the mildness, the conciliating forbearance, the lively and never-failing tenderness of affection, which every branch of his behaviour towards his partner ought to display; and of the readiness with which he ought to make large sacrifices of personal inclination, ease, and interest, when essential to her permanent welfare. "Husbands, love your wives, and be not bitter against them," "Ye husbands, dwell with your wives according to knowledge; giving honour unto the wife, as unto the weaker vessel," "Husbands, love your wives, as Christ also loved the Church, and gave himself for it." If a woman marry a person without having sufficient reason to be satisfied, from actual knowledge of his character, that the commands of the Scriptures will decide his general conduct, the fault surely is her own.

The foundation of the greater portion of the unhappiness which clouds matrimonial life, is to be sought in the unconcern so prevalent in the world, as to those radical principles on which character and the permanence of character depend, – the principles of religion. Popular language indicates the state of popular opinion. If an union about to take place, or recently contracted, between two young persons, be mentioned in conversation; the first question which we hear asked concerning it is, whether it be a **good match**. The very countenance and voice of the inquirer, and of the answerer, the terms of the answer returned, and the observations, whether expressive of satisfaction or regret, which fall from

33

the lips of the company present in the circle, all concur to shew what, in common estimation, is meant by being well married. If a young woman be described as thus married, the terms imply, that she is united to a man whose station and fortune are such, when compared with her own or those of her parents, that in point of precedence, in point of command of finery and of money, she is, more or less, a gainer by the bargain. In high life they imply, that she will now possess the enviable advantages of taking place of other ladies in the neighbourhood; of decking herself out with jewels and lace; of inhabiting splendid apartments; rolling in handsome carriages; gazing on numerous servants in gaudy liveries: and of going to London, and other fashionable scenes of resort, all in a degree somewhat higher than that in which a calculating broker, after poring on her pedigree, summing up her property in hand, and computing, at the market place, what is contingent or in reversion, would have pronounced her entitled to them. A few slight and obvious alterations would adapt the picture to the middle classes of society. But what do the terms imply as to the character of the man selected to be her husband? Probably nothing. His character is a matter which seldom enters into the consideration of the persons who use them, unless it, at length, appears in the shape of an after-thought, or is awkwardly hitched into their remarks for the sake of decorum. If the terms imply any thing on this point, they mean no more than that he is not scandalously and notoriously addicted to vice. He may be covetous, he may be proud, he may be ambitious, he may be malignant, he may be devoid of Christian principles, practice, and belief; or, to say the very least, it may be totally unknown whether he does not fall, in every particular, under this description; and yet, in the language and in the opinion of the generality of both sexes, the match is excellent. In like manner a diminution of power as to the supposed advantages already enumerated, though counterpoised by the acquisition of a companion eminent for his virtues, is supposed to constitute a bad match; and is universally lamented in polite meetings with real or affected concern. The good or bad fortune of a young man in the choice of a wife is estimated according to the same rules.

From those who contract marriages, either chiefly or in a considerable degree, through motives of interest or of ambition, it would be folly to expect previous solicitude respecting piety of heart. And it would be equal folly to expect that such marriages, however they may answer the purposes of interest or of ambition, should terminate otherwise than in wretchedness. Wealth may be secured; rank may be obtained; but if wealth and rank are to be main ingredients in the cup of matrimonial felicity, the pure and sweet wine will be exhausted at once, and nothing remain but bitter and corrosive dregs. When attachments are free from the contamination of such unworthy motives, it by no means always follows that much attention is paid to intrinsic excellence of moral and religious character. Affection, quick-sighted in discerning, and diligent in scrutinising, the minutest circumstances which contribute to shew whether it is met with reciprocal sincerity and ardor, is, in other respects, purblind and inconsiderate. It magnifies good qualities which exist; it seems to itself to perceive merits which, to other eyes, are invisible; it gives credit for what it wishes to discover; it enquires not, where it fears a disappointment. It forgets that the spirit of the scriptural command "not to be yoked unequally with unbelievers," a command reiterated in other parts of holy writ, may justly be deemed to extend to all cases, in which there is reason to apprehend that religion is not the great operative principle in the mind of the man. Yet on what grounds can a woman hope for the blessing of God on a marriage contracted without regard to his injunctions? What security can she have for happiness, as depending on the conduct of her husband, if the only foundation on which confidence can be safely reposed, be wanting? And ought she not, in common prudence, to consider it as wanting, until she is thoroughly convinced of its existence? He whose ruling principle is that of stedfast obedience to the laws of God, has a pledge to give, and it is a pledge worthy of being trusted, that he will discharge his duties to his fellow-creatures, according to the different relations in which he may be placed. Every other bond of confidence is brittle as a thread, and looks specious only to prove delusive. A woman who receives for her husband a person of whose moral and religious character she knows no more than that it is outwardly decent, stakes her welfare upon a very hazardous experiment. She who marries a man not entitled even to that humble praise, in the hope of reclaiming him, stakes it on an experiment in which there is scarcely a chance of her success.

Among various absurd and mischievous lessons which young women were accustomed in the last age to learn from dramatic representations, one of the most absurd and mischievous was this; that a man of vicious character was very easily reformed; and that he was particularly likely, when once reformed, to make a desirable and exemplary husband. At the conclusion of almost every comedy the hero of the piece, signalized throughout its progress by qualities and conduct radically incompatible with the existence of matrimonial happiness, was introduced upon the stage as having experienced a sudden change of heart, and become a convert, as by a miracle, to the ways of religion and virtue. The same preposterous reformation occasionally finds a place in compositions of modern date. The reasons which have induced many writers, by no means unskilled in the science of human nature, to construct their dramas on a plan so unnatural, are evident. Following the bent of his own contaminated mind, or solicitous only to suit the taste of a corrupted audience, the author conceived immorality seasoned with wit to furnish the most copious and attractive fund of entertainment. He formed his plot, drew his characters, and arranged his incidents, accordingly. His catastrophe was to turn on the usual hinge, marriage. But though he had, without scruple, exhibited his hero through four entire acts, and three quarters of the fifth, as unprincipled; yet in the final scene to unite him unprincipled as he was to the lady of his wishes, a lady whom it had been found convenient to represent throughout the drama in a much more respectable light than her intended husband, was an indecorum too flagrant to be hazarded. For form's sake, therefore, it was necessary that a reformation, and through want of time that an instantaneous reformation, should be supposed to be wrought in his heart. Let the female sex be assured, that whenever on the stage of real life an irreligious and immoral young man is suddenly found, on the eve of matrimony, to change his external conduct, and to recommend himself by professions of a determination to amend; the probability that the change is adopted, as in the theatre, for the sake of form and convenience, and that it will not be durable after the purposes of form and convenience shall have been answered by it, is one of those which approach the nearest to certainty.

The truths which have been inculcated as furnishing the only foundation for rational hopes of happiness in marriage are such as ought to be established in the mind, while the affections are yet unengaged. When the heart has received an impression, reason acts feebly or treacherously. But let not the recent impression be permitted to sink deeper, ere the habitual principles and conduct of him who has made it shall have been ascertained. On these points in particular, points which a young woman cannot herself possess adequate means of investigating, let the advice and inquiries of virtuous relatives be solicited. Let not their opinions, though the purport of them should prove unacceptable, be undervalued; nor their remonstrances, if they should remonstrate, be construed as unkindness. Let it be remembered that, although parental authority can never be justified in constraining a daughter to marry against her will; there are many cases in which it may be justified in requiring her to pause. Let it be remembered that, if she should unite herself to a man who is not under the habitual influence of Christianity, unsettled as to its principles, or careless as to some of its practical duties; she has to dread not only the risk of personal unhappiness from his conduct towards her, but the dangerous contagion of intimate example. She has to dread that his irreligion may infect herself, his unsteadiness may render her unsteady, his carelessness may teach her to be careless. Does the scene appear in prospect gloomy or ambiguous? Let her be wise, let her exert herself, before it is too late. It is better to encounter present anxiety, than to avoid it at the expence of greater and durable evils. And even if affection has already acquired such force, as not to be repressed without very painful struggles; let her be consoled and animated by the consciousness that the sacrifice is to prevent, while prevention is yet in her power, years of danger and of misery; that it is an act not only of ultimate kindness to herself, but of duty to God; and that every act of humble and persevering duty may hope to receive, in a better world, a reward proportioned to the severity of the trial,

In a union so intimate as that of matrimonial life those diversities in temper, habits and inclinations, which in a less close connection might not have been distinctly perceived, or would have attracted notice but seldom, unavoidably swell into importance. Hence, among the qualifications which influence the probability of connubial comfort, a general similarity of disposition between the two parties is one of especial moment. Where strong affection prevails, a spirit of accommodation will prevail also. But it is not desirable that the spirit of accommodation should be subjected to rigorous or very frequent experiments. Great disparity in age between a husband and a wife, or a wide difference in rank antecedently to marriage, is, on this account, liable to be productive of disquietude. The sprightliness of youth seems levity, and the sobriety of maturer years to be tinctured with moroseness, when closely contrasted. A sudden introduction to affluence, a sudden and great elevation in the scale of society, are apt to intoxicate; and a sudden reduction in outward appearance to be felt as degrading. Instances, however, are not very rare in which the force of affection, of good sense, and of good principles, shews itself permanently superior to the influence of causes, which, to minds less happily attempered, and less under the guidance of religious motives, prove sources of anxiety and vexation.

To delude a young man by encouraging his attentions for the pleasure of exhibiting him as a conquest, for the purpose of exciting the assiduities of another person, or from any motive except the impulse of mutual regard, is a proceeding too plainly repugnant to justice, and to delicacy of sentiment, to require much observation. On such subjects, even inadvertence is highly culpable. What, then is the guilt of her who deliberately raises hopes which she is resolved not to fulfil?

There remains yet another caution relating to the present subject, which appears worthy of being suggested. A young woman, unbiased by interested motives, is sometimes led to contract a matrimonial engagement without suspecting that she perhaps does not entertain for her intended husband the warm and rooted affection necessary for the conservation of connubial happiness. She beholds him with general approbation; she is conscious that there is no other person whom she prefers to him: she receives lively pleasure from his attentions: and she imagines that she loves him with tenderness and ardour. Yet it is very possible that she may be unacquainted with the real state of her heart. Thoughtless inexperience, gentleness of disposition, the quick susceptibility of early youth, and chiefly perhaps the complacency which all persons, whose affections are not pre-occupied, feel towards those who distinguish them by particular proofs of regard, may have excited an indistinct partiality which she mistakes for rivetted attachment. Many an unhappy wife has discovered the mistake too late.

It is highly desirable that a young woman as soon as ever she receives particular attentions from an individual of the other sex, should communicate with perfect openness the circumstance to her parents. And every young woman ought habitually to reflect, that her first object should not be to be settled in matrimonial life, but to be prepared to do her duty in any situation in which Providence may design her to be placed.

Love and Marriage
(A Father's Legacy to His
Daughters – John Gregory, 1761)

...Thousands of women of the best hearts and finest parts, have been ruined by men who approach them under the specious name of friendship. But supposing a man to have the most undoubted honour, yet his friendship to a woman is so near akin to love, that if she be very agreeable in her person, she will probably very soon find a lover, where she only wished to meet a friend. Let me here, however, warn you against that weakness so common among vain women, the imagination that every man who takes particular notice of them is a lover. Nothing can expose you more to ridicule, than the taking up a man on the suspicion of being your lover, who perhaps never once thought of you in that view, and giving yourselves those airs so common among silly women on such occasions.

There is a kind of unmeaning gallantry much practised by some men, which, if you have any discernment, you will find really very harmless. Men of this sort will attend you to public places, and be useful to you by a number of little observations, which those of a superior class do not so much understand, or have no leisure to regard, or perhaps are too proud to submit to. Look on the compliments of such men, as words of course, which they repeat to every agreeable woman of their acquaintance. There is a familiarity they are apt to assume, which a proper dignity in your behaviour will be easily able to check.

There is a different species of men, whom you may like as agreeable companions, men of worth, taste, and genius, whose conversation, in some respects, may be superior to what you generally meet with among your own sex. It will be

Elinor turned involuntarily to Marianne, to see whether it could be unobserved by her. At that moment she first perceived him; and her whole countenance glowing with sudden delight, she would have moved towards him instantly, had not her sister caught hold of her. "Good heavens," she exclaimed, "he is there – he is there! – Oh why does he not look at me? Why cannot I speak to him?" "Pray, pray be composed," cried Elinor, "and do not betray what you feel to everybody present. Perhaps he has not observed you yet."

foolish in you to deprive yourselves of an useful and agreeable acquaintance, merely because idle people say he is your lover. Such a man may like your company without having any design on your person.

People whose sentiments, and particularly whose tastes correspond, naturally like to associate together, although neither of them have the most distant view of any further connection. But as this similarity of minds often gives rise to a more tender attachment than friendship, it will be prudent to keep a watchful eye over yourselves, lest your hearts become too far engaged before you are aware of it. At the same time, I do not think, that your sex, at least in this part of the world, have much of that sensibility which disposes to such attachments. What is commonly called love among you, is rather gratitude, and a partiality to the man who prefers you to the rest of your sex, and such a man you often marry, with little either of personal esteem or affection. Indeed, without an unusual share of natural sensibility, and very peculiar good fortune, a woman in this country has very little probability of marrying for love.

It is a maxim laid down among you, and a very prudent one it is, That love is not to begin on your part, but is entirely to be the consequence of our attachment to you. Now, supposing a woman to have sense and taste, she will not find many men to whom she can possibly be supposed to bear any considerable share of esteem. Among these few it is a very great chance if any of them distinguishes her particularly. Love, at least with us, is exceedingly capricious, and will not always fix where reason says it should. But supposing one of them should become particularly attached to her, it is extremely improbable that he should be the man in the world her heart most approved of.

As, therefore, Nature has not given that unlimited range in your choice, which we enjoy, she has wisely and benevolently assigned to you a greater flexibility of taste on this subject. Some agreeable qualities recommend a gentleman to your common good liking and friendship. In the course of his acquaintance, he contracts an attachment to you. When you perceive it, it excites your gratitude; this gratitude rises into a preference, and this preference perhaps at last advances to some degree of attachment; especially if it meets with crosses and difficulties; for these, and a state of suspense, are very great incitements to attachment and are the food of love, in both sexes. If attachment was not excited in your sex in this manner, there is not one of a million of you that could ever marry with any degree of love.

A man of taste and delicacy marries a woman because he loves her more than any other. A woman of equal taste and delicacy marries him, because she esteems him, and because he gives her that preference. But if a man unfortunately becomes attached to a woman whose heart is secretly pre-engaged, his attachment, instead of obtaining a suitable return, is particularly offensive; and if he persists to teaze her, he makes himself equally the object of her scorn and aversion.

The effects of love among men are diversified by their different tempers. An artful man may counterfeit every one of them so as easily to impose on a young girl, of an open generous and feeling heart, if she is not extremely on her guard. The finest parts in such a girl may not always prove sufficient for her security. The dark and crooked paths of cunning are unsearchable and inconceivable to an honourable and elevated mind.

The following, I apprehend, are the most genuine effects of an honourable passion among the men, and the most difficult to counterfeit. A man of delicacy often betrays his passion by his too great anxiety to conceal it, especially if he has little hopes of success. True love in all its stages seeks concealment, and never expects success. It renders a man not only respectful but timid to the highest degree in his behaviour to the woman he loves. To conceal the awe he stands in of her, he may sometimes affect pleasantry, but it sits aukwardly on him, and he quickly relapses into seriousness, if not into dulness. He magnifies all her real perfections in his imagination, and is either blind to her failings, or converts them into beauties. Like a person conscious of guilt; he is jealous that every eye observes him, and to avoid this, he shuns all the little observances of common gallantry.

His heart and his character will be improved in every respect by his attachment. His manners will become more gentle, and his conversation more agreeable; but diffidence and embarrassment will always make him appear to disadvantage in the company of his mistress. If the fascination continue long, it will totally depress his spirits, and extinguish every active, vigorous, and manly principle of his mind. You will find this subject beautifully and pathetically painted in Thomson's Spring.

When you observe in a gentleman's behaviour these marks which I have described above, reflect seriously what you are to do. If his attachment is agreeable to you, I leave you to do as nature, good sense, and delicacy shall direct you. If you love him, let me advise you never to discover to him the full extent of your love, no not although you marry him. That sufficiently shews your preference, which is all he is entitled to know. If he has delicacy, he will ask no stronger proof of your affection for your sake; if he has sense he will not ask it for his own. This is an unpleasant truth, but it is my duty to let you know it. Violent love cannot subsist, at least cannot be expressed, for any time together on both sides; otherwise the certain consequence, however concealed, is satiety and disgust. Nature in this case, has laid the reserve on you.

If you see evident proofs of a gentleman's attachment, and are determined to shut your heart against him, as you ever hope to be used with generosity by the person who may engage your own heart, treat him honourably and humanely. Do not let him linger in a miserable suspense, but be anxious to let him know your sentiments with regard to him.

However people's hearts may deceive them, there is scarcely a person that can love for any time without at least some distant hope of success. If you really wish to undeceive a lover, you may do it in a variety of ways. There is a certain species of easy familiarity in your behaviour, which may satisfy him, if he has any discernment left, that he has nothing to hope for. But perhaps your particular temper may not admit of this. You may easily shew that you want to avoid his company; but if he is a man whose friendship you wish to preserve, you may not choose this method, because then you lose him in every capacity. You may get a common friend to explain matters to him, or fall on many other devices, if you are seriously anxious to put him out of suspense.

But if you are resolved against every such method, at least do not shun opportunities of letting him explain himself. If you do this, you act barbarously and unjustly. If he brings you to an explanation, give him a polite but resolute, and decisive answer. In whatever way you convey your sentiments to him, if he is a man of spirit and delicacy, he will give you no further trouble, nor apply to your friends for their intercession. This last is a method of courtship which every man of spirit will disdain. He will never whine nor sue for your pity. That would mortify him almost as much as your scorn. In short, you may possibly break such a heart, but you can never bend it. – Great pride always accompanies delicate minds, however concealed under the appearance of the utmost gentleness and modesty, and is the passion of all others the most difficult to conquer.

There is a case where a woman may coquet justifiably to the utmost verge which her conscience will allow. It is where a gentleman purposely declines to make his addresses, till such time as he thinks himself perfectly sure of her consent. This at the bottom is intended to force a woman to give up the undoubted privilege of her sex, the privilege of refusing; it is intended to force her to explain herself, in effect, before the gentleman deigns to do it, and by this means oblige her to violate the modesty and delicacy of her sex, and to invert the clearest order of nature. All this sacrifice is proposed to be made, merely to gratify a most despicable vanity, in a man who would degrade the very woman whom he wishes to make his wife.

It is of great importance to distinguish, whether a gentleman who has the appearance of being your lover, delays to speak explicitly, from the motive I have mentioned, or from a diffidence inseparable from true attachment. In the one case you can scarcely use him too ill; in the other, you ought to use him with great kindness; and the greatest kindness you can shew him, if you are determined not to listen to his addresses, is to let him know it as soon as possible.

I know the many excuses with which women endeavour to justify themselves to the world, and to their own consciences, when they act otherwise. Sometimes they plead ignorance, or at least uncertainty, of the gentleman's real sentiments. That may sometimes be the case. -Sometimes they plead the decorum of their sex, which enjoins an equal behaviour to all men, and forbids them to consider any man as a lover till he has directly told them so. Perhaps few women carry their ideas of female delicacy and decorum so far as I do. But I must say you are not entitled to plead the obligation of these virtues, in opposition to the superior ones of gratitude, justice and humanity. The man is entitled to all these, who prefers you to the rest of your sex, and perhaps whose greatest weakness is this very preference. The truth of the matter is, vanity and the love of admiration is so prevailing a passion among you, that you may be considered to make a very great sacrifice, till you give up a lover, whenever every art of coquetry fails to keep him, or till he forces you to an explanation. You can be fond of the love, when you are indifferent to, or even when you despise the lover.

But the deepest and most artful coquetry is employed by women of superior taste and sense, to engage and fix the heart of a man whom the world and whom they themselves esteem, although they are firmly determined never to marry him. But his conversation amuses them, and his attachment is the highest gratification to their vanity; nay, they can sometimes be gratified with the utter ruin of his fortune, fame, and happiness. God forbid I should ever think so of all your sex! I know many of them have principles, have generosity and dignity of soul that elevates them above the worthless vanity I have been speaking of.

Such a woman, I am persuaded, may always convert a lover, if she cannot give him her affections, into a warm and steady friend, provided he is a man of sense, resolution, and candour. If she explains herself to him with a generous openness and freedom, he must feel the stroke as a man; but he will likewise bear it as a man; what he suffers he will suffer in silence. Every sentiment of esteem will remain; but love, though it requires very little food, and is easily surfeited with too much, yet it requires some. He will view her in the light of a married woman; and though passion subsides, yet a man of a candid and generous heart, always retains a tenderness for a woman he has once loved, and who has used him well, beyond what he feels for any other of her sex.

If he has not confided his own secrets to any body, he has an undoubted title to ask you not to divulge it. If a woman chooses to trust any of her companions with her own unfortunate attachments, she may, as it is her own affair alone; but if she has any generosity or gratitude, she will not betray a secret which does not belong to her.

Male coquetry is much less inexcusable than female, as well as more pernicious; but it is rare in this country. Very few men will give themselves the trouble to gain or retain any woman's affections, unless they have views on them either of an honourable or dishonourable kind. Men employed in the pursuit of business, ambition, or pleasure, will not give themselves the trouble to engage a woman's affections merely from the vanity of conquest, and of triumphing over the heart of an innocent and defenceless girl. Besides people never value much what is entirely in their power. A man of parts, sentiments, and address, if he lays aside all regard to truth and humanity, may engage the hearts of fifty women at the same time, and may likewise conduct his coquetry with so much art, as to put it out of the power of any of them to specify a single expression which could be said to be directly expressive of love. This ambiguity of behaviour, this art of keeping one in suspense, is the greatest secret of coquetry in both sexes. It is the more cruel in us, because we can carry it to what length we please, without your being so much as at liberty to complain or expostulate; whereas we can break our chain, and force you to explain, whenever we become impatient of our situation.

I have insisted the more particularly on this subject of courtship, because it may most readily happen to you, at that early period of life, when you can have little experience or knowledge of the world; when your passions are warm, and your judgements not arrived at such full maturity as to be able to correct them;- I wish you to possess such high principles of honour and generosity, as will render you incapable of deceiving, and at the same time to possess that acute discernment which may secure you against being deceived.

A woman, in this country, may easily prevent the first impressions of love; and every motive of prudence and delicacy should make her guard her heart against them, till such time as she has received the most convincing proofs of the attachment of a man of such merit, as will justify a reciprocal regard. Your hearts, indeed, may be shut inflexibly and permanently, against all the merit a man can possess. That may be your misfortune, but cannot be your fault. In such a situation, you would be equally unjust to yourselves and to your lover, if you gave him your hand when your heart revolted against him. But miserable will be your fate, if you allow an attachment to steal on you before you are sure of a return; or, what is infinitely worse, where there are wanting those qualities which alone can ensure happiness in a married state.

I know nothing that renders a woman more despicable than her thinking it essential to happiness to be married. Besides the gross indelicacy of the sentiment, it is a false one, as thousands of women have experienced. But if it was true, the belief that it is so, and the consequent impatience to be married, is the most effectual way to prevent it.

You must not think from this, that I do not wish you to marry. On the contrary, I am of opinion, that you may attain a superior degree of happiness in a married state, to what you can possibly find in any other. I know the forlorn and unprotected situation of an old maid, the chagrin and peevishness which are apt to infect their tempers, and the great difficulty of making a transition with dignity and cheerfulness, from the period of youth, beauty, admiration, and respect, into the calm, silent, unnoticed retreat of declining years.

I see some unmarried women of active vigorous minds, and great vivacity of spirits, degrading themselves; sometimes by entering into a dissipated course of life, unsuitable to their years, and exposing themselves to the ridicule of girls, who might have been their grand-children; sometimes by oppressing their acquaintances by impertinent intrusions into their private affairs; and sometimes by being propagators of scandal and defamation. All this is owing to an exuberant activity of spirit, which if it had found employment at home, would have rendered them respectable and useful members of society.

I see other women, in the same situation, gentle, modest, blessed with sense, taste, delicacy, and every milder feminine virtue of the heart, but of weak spirits, bashful, and timid; I see such women sinking into obscurity and insignificance, and gradually losing every elegant accomplishment; for this evident reason, that they are not united to a partner who has sense, and worth, and taste, to know their value; one who is not able to draw forth their concealed qualities, and shew them to advantage; who can give that support to their feeble spirits which they stand so much in need of; and who, by his affection and tenderness, might make such a woman happy in exerting every talent and accomplishing herself in every elegant art that could contribute to his amusement.

In short, I am of opinion, that a married state, if entered into from proper motives of esteem and affection, will be the happiest for yourselves, make you most respectable in the eyes of the world, and the most useful members of society. But I confess I am not enough of a patriot to wish you to marry for the good of the public. I wish you to marry for no other reason but to make yourselves happier. When I am so particular in my advices about your conduct, I own my heart beats with the fond hope of making you worthy the attachment of men who will deserve you, and be sensible of your merit. But Heaven forbid you should ever relinquish the ease and independence of a single life, to become the slaves of a fool or a tyrant's caprice.

As these have always been my sentiments, I shall do but justice, when I leave you in such independent circumstances as may lay you under no temptation to do from necessity what you would never do from choice. – This will likewise save you from that cruel mortification to a woman of spirit, the suspicion that a gentleman thinks he does you an honour or a favour when he asks you for his wife.

If I live till you arrive at that age when you shall be capable to judge for yourselves, and do not strangely alter my sentiments, I shall act towards you in a very different manner from what most parents do. My opinion has always been, that when that period arrives, the parental authority ceases.

I hope I shall always treat you with that affection and easy confidence which may dispose you to look on me as your friend. In that capacity alone I shall think myself entitled to give you my opinion; in the doing of which, I should think myself highly criminal, if I did not to the utmost of my power endeavour to divest myself of all personal vanity, and all prejudices in favour of my particular taste. If you did not chuse to follow my advice, I should not on that account cease to love you as my children. Though my right to your obedience was expired, yet I should think nothing could release me from the ties of nature and humanity.

You may perhaps imagine, that the reserved behaviour which I recommend to you, and your appearing seldom at public places, must cut off all opportunities of your being acquainted with gentlemen. I am very far from intending this. I advise you to no reserve, but what will render you more respected and beloved by our sex. I do not think public places suited to make people acquainted together. They can only be distinguished there by their looks and external behaviour. But it is in private companies alone where you can expect easy and agreeable conversation, which I should never wish you to decline. If you do not allow gentlemen to become acquainted with you, you can never expect to marry with attachment on either side. – Love is very seldom produced at first sight; at least it must have, in that case, a very unjustifiable foundation. True love is founded on esteem, in a correspondence of tastes and sentiments, and steals on the heart imperceptibly.

There is one advice I shall leave you, to which I beg your particular attention. Before your affections come to be in the least engaged to any man, examine your tempers, your tastes, and your hearts, very severely, and settle in your own minds what are the requisites to your happiness in a married state; and as it is almost impossible that you should get every thing you wish, come to a steady determination what you are to consider as essential, and what may be sacrificed.

If you have hearts disposed by Nature for love and friendship, and possess those feelings which enable you to enter into all the refinements and delicacies of these attachments, consider well, for Heaven's sake, and as you value your future happiness, before you give them any indulgence. If you have the misfortune (for a very great misfortune it commonly is to your sex) to have such a temper and such sentiments deeply rooted in you, if you have spirit and resolution to resist the solicitations of vanity, the persecution of friends, (for you will have lost the only friend that would never persecute you) and can support the prospect of the many inconveniences attending the state of an old maid, which I formerly pointed out, then you may indulge yourselves in that kind of sentimental reading and conversation which is most correspondent to your feelings.

But if you find, on a strict self-examination, that marriage is absolutely essential to your happiness, keep the secret inviolable in your own bosoms, for the reason I formerly mentioned; but shun, as you would do the most fatal poison, all that species of reading and conversation which warms the imagination, which engages and softens the heart, and raises the taste above the level of common life. If you do otherwise, consider the terrible conflict of passions this may afterwards raise in your breasts.

If this refinement once takes deep root in your minds, and you do not obey its dictates, but marry from vulgar and mercenary views, you may never be able to eradicate it entirely, and then it will embitter all your married days. Instead of meeting with sense delicacy, tenderness, a lover, a friend, an equal companion, in a husband, you may be tired with insipidity and dullness; shocked with indelicacy, or mortified by indifference. You will find none to compassionate, or even understand your sufferings; for your husbands may not use you cruelly, and may give you as much money for your cloaths, personal expence, and domestic necessaries, as is suitable to their fortunes. The world would therefore look on you as unreasonable women, and who did not deserve to be happy, if you were not so – To avoid these complicated evils, if you are determined at all events to marry, I would advise you to make all your reading and amusements of such a kind as do not effect the heart, nor the imagination, except in the way of wit and humour.

I have no view by these advices to lead your tastes; I only want to persuade you of the necessity of knowing your own minds, which, though seemingly very easy, is what your sex seldom attain on many important occasions in life, but particularly on this of which I am speaking. There is not a quality I more anxiously wish you to possess, than that collected decisive spirit which rests on itself, which enables you to see where your true happiness lies, and to pursue it with the most determined resolution. In matters of business, follow the advice of those who know them better than yourselves, and in whose integrity you can confide; but in matters of taste, that depend on your own feelings, consult no one friend whatever, but consult your own hearts.

If a gentleman makes his addresses to you, or gives you reason to believe he will do so, before you allow your affections to be engaged, endeavour, in the most prudent and secret manner, to procure from your friends every necessary piece of information concerning him; such as his character for sense, his morals, his temper, fortune and family,; whether it is distinguished for parts and worth, or folly, knavery, and loathsome hereditary diseases. When your friends inform you of these they have fulfilled their duty. If they go further, they have not that deference for you which a becoming dignity on your part would effectually command.

Whatever your views are in marrying, take every possible precaution to prevent their being disappointed. If fortune, and the pleasures it brings, are your aim, it is not sufficient that the settlements of a jointure and children's provisions be ample, and properly secured; it is necessary you should enjoy the fortune during your own life. The principal security you can have for this will depend on your marrying a good-natured generous man, who despises money, and who will let you live where you can best enjoy that pleasure, that pomp and the parade of life for which you married him.

From what I have said, you will easily see, that I could never pretend to advise whom you should marry; but I can with great confidence advise whom you should not marry.

Avoid a companion that may entail any hereditary disease on your posterity, particularly (that most dreadful of all human calamities) madness. It is the height of imprudence to run into such a danger, and, in my opinion, highly criminal.

Do not marry a fool; he is the most untractable of all animals; he is led by his passions and caprices, and is incapable of hearing the voice of reason. It may probably, too, hurt your vanity to have husbands for whom you have reason to blush and tremble every time they open their lips in company. But the worst circumstance that attends a fool, is his constant jealousy of his wife being thought to govern him. This renders it impossible to lead him; and he is continually doing absurd and disagreeable things, for, no other reason but to shew he dares to do them.

A rake is always a suspicious husband, because he has only known the most worthless of your sex. He likewise entails the worst of diseases on his wife and children, if he has the misfortune to have any.

If you have a sense of religion yourselves, do not think of husbands who have none. If they have tolerable understandings, they will be glad that you have religion, for their own sakes, and for the sake of their families; but it will sink you in their esteem. If they are weak men, they will be continually teasing and shocking you about your principles. – If you have children, you will suffer the most bitter distress, in seeing all your endeavours to form their minds to virtue and piety, all your endeavours to secure their present and eternal happiness frustrated, and turned into ridicule.

As I look on your choice of a husband to be of the greatest consequence to your happiness, I hope you will make it with the utmost circumspection. Do not give way to a sudden sally of passion, and dignify it with the name of love. – Genuine love is not founded in caprice; it is founded in nature, on honourable views, on virtue, on similarity of tastes and sympathy of souls.

If you have these sentiments, you will never marry anyone, when you are not in that situation, in point of fortune, which is necessary to the happiness of either of you. What that competency may be, can only be determined by your own tastes. It would be ungenerous in you to take advantage of a lover's attachment, to plunge him into distress; and if he has any honour, no personal gratification will ever tempt him to enter into any connection which will render you unhappy. If you have as much between you as to satisfy all your demands, it is sufficient.

I shall conclude with endeavouring to remove a difficulty which must naturally occur to any woman of reflection on the subject of marriage. What is to become of all these refinements of delicacy, that dignity of manners, which checked all familiarities, and suspended desire in respectful and awful admiration? In answer to this, I shall only observe, that if motives of interest and vanity have had any share in your resolutions to marry, none of these chimerical notions will give you any pain; nay, they will very quickly appear as ridiculous in your own eyes, as they probably always did in the eyes of your husbands. They have been sentiments which have floated in your imaginations, but have never reached your hearts. But if these sentiments have been truly genuine, and if you have had the singular happy fate to attach those who understood them, you have no reason to be afraid.

Marriage, indeed, will at once dispel the enchantment raised by external beauty; but the virtues and graces that first warmed the heart, that reserve and delicacy which always left the lover something further to wish, and often made him doubtful of your sensibility or attachment, may and ought ever to remain. The tumult of passion will necessarily subside; but it will be succeeded by an endearment that affects the heart in a more equal, more sensible, and tender manner. – But I must check myself, and not indulge in descriptions that may mislead you, and that too sensibly awake the remembrance of my happier days which, perhaps, it were better for me to forget forever.

I have thus given you my opinion on some of the most important articles of your future life, chiefly calculated for that period when you are just entering the world. I have endeavoured to avoid some peculiarities of opinion, which, from their contradiction to the general practice of the world, I might reasonably have suspected were not so well founded. But in writing to you, I am afraid my heart has been too full, and too warmly interested, to allow me to keep this resolution. This may have produced some embarrassment, and some seeming contradictions. What I have written has been the amusement of some solitary hours, and has served to divert some melancholly reflections. – I am conscious I undertook a task to which I was very unequal but I have discharged a part of my duty. – You will at least be pleased with it, as the last mark of your father's love and attention.

Advice in the Time of Courtship
(*A Letter of Genteel and Moral Advice to a Young Lady* – Wetenhall Wilkes, 1741)

… As Love Addresses are either expected by or impos'd on all your Sex, a few Cautions to be us'd in the Time of Courtship may deserve a place among my other Precepts. Give me leave upon this Occasion to recollect some Remarks which I have met with in Discourse, and to compare them with what falls under my own Observation.

I have heard a Lady of nice Discernment say, that "Nothing is more dangerous to a Female than the Vanity of Conquests, and that it is as safe to play with Fire as to dally with Gallantry." That this Lady collected the Phrase from Experience, it would be ungenerous to suspect, but hence it may be infer'd that a young Lady conspires against her own Safety and Honour, who is over free of Temper, forward in talking, or fond of being thought witty in the Presence of her Courtier. Except Wit be temper'd with Discretion and ripen'd by Experience; improv'd by Reading, and guarded by Judgment, it is the most dangerous Companion that can lurk in a Female Bosom. It softens her Sentiments, makes her fond of being politely addrest, curious of fine Speeches; impatient of Praise; and exposes her to all the Temptations of Flattery and Deceit. Ladies have great reason to be cautious and watchful over themselves; for even to listen to Compliments and gay Addresses may betray them into Weakness and Indiscretion.

Be careful how you give Way to what many Ladies call an "innocent Liberty", for here Civility may be taken for an Invitation. The double Temptation of Vanity and Desire is so prevalent in our Sex, that we are apt to interpret every obliging

"Well, my dear," said Mrs Jennings," and how did you travel?"
"Not in the stage, I assure you," replied Miss Steele, with quick
exultation; "we came post all the way, and had a very smart beau to
attend us. Dr Davies was coming to town, and so we thought we'd
join him in a postchaise; and he behaved very genteelly, and paid ten
or twelve shillings more than we did."

Look, Gesture, Smile or Sentence of a Female we like to the hopeful Side. Therefore let your Deportment forbid without Rudeness, and oblige without Invitation. We look upon a Woman's Eyes to be the Interpreters of her Heart, and we often gather more Encouragement from a pleasing Glance than from her softest Words. The Language of the Eyes is very significant.

Never fix your liking on any Man that has not those good Qualities which you have labour'd after yourself, and who is not likely to be a Friend to Virtue.

When a Lady is addrest by her Votary, let his Proposals be ever so honourable, she ought to be Cautious how she places her Affections. She should carry herself with an even Temper, and keep herself at a genteel Distance, lest the Conquest afterwards might be reckon'd cheap. An early Fondness often suffers.

As the Intentions are not legible, the World is apt to judge of Persons by their Behaviour, Conversation and Appearances. If all young Ladies were conscious of this, surely they would be more circumspect and reserv'd than to allow such Liberties as are too often us'd in Love-Addresses. They may suppose them to be Characters of Love and Passion; but in the End such mistaken Indulgences often destroy all that Esteem which their Lovers might have for them, if they were not quite so tractable. Easy Compliances extinguish the Desire of Marriage, and make the fair Sex only consider'd as Subjects of Gallantry and Amusement.

Be not over credulous in believing every obliging Thing your Admirer says; for that would expose you to his Artillery of Persuasions. When he praises your Beauty, Wit, Shape or Temper, and tells you that in his Eyes, you excel all others of your Sex, do not receive such Compliments as an

Homage due to your Merit, without examining whether he be sincere or flatters. The Lives of some men are a meer Commerce of Compliments and Dissimulation to impose upon female Softness; and this often makes Credulity in Women as infamous as Falsehood is reproachful in Men. All the Havoc which is made in the Habitations of Beauty and Innocence by the Arts and Gallantries of crafty Men, is owing altogether to this female Weakness. Too often Credulity is overtaken by Disgrace.

There are two general Answers may be given by any of the Fair to the Fop or the Courtier, which in all Cases will dismiss either with his Impertinences to her Credit and Satisfaction. If a Fop or Beau says an obliging Thing to you, with a mild indifferent Air receive it, and return him Thanks; but if he insists upon fulsome Compliments, give him to understand his favours are misplac'd, that such Discourse makes you uneasy, and that you hope his good Manners will direct him to wave it. If your Spark be troublesome, modestly reprove his Boldness, shew a dislike to his Familiarities, and with a courteous inoffensive Air, forbid him all unseasonable Visits, and private Retirements. If you are warmly importun'd, let him know that you are under the Direction of a Parent and Relations, that you are not at your own Disposal, and that you have resolv'd not to dispose of yourself. All this must be done without Pettishness, Peevishness, or Disdain, lest your disappointed Teazer should, inflam'd with Resentment and Revenge, spread Reports injurious to your Honour. Opportunities should be avoided as much as possible. Great is the Danger that a Female incurs, let her imagine her Simplicity and Innocnce to be ever so invincible, by too much Familiarity with a male Companion. She that wonders what People mean by Temptations, that thinks herself secure against all Attacks, and defies Mankind to do their worst, depends too much on her own Sufficiency, and may be surpriz'd into Weakness and Deceit. Whoever is made of Flesh and Blood is subject to human Frailties; wherefore it must be much safer to fly from, than to fight with what the World calls "Opportunities" and Religion "Temptations". Thousands of your Sex have been gradually betray'd from innocent Freedoms to Ruin and Infamy, and thousands of our Sex have begun with Flatteries, Protestations and Endearments, but ended with Reproaches, Perjury and Perfidiousness. She that considers this will shun like Death, such Baits of Guilt and Misery, and be very cautious to whom she listens. When a Man talks of honourable Love, you may with an honest Pleasure hear his Story, but, if he flies into Raptures, calls you an Angel or a Goddess, vows to stab himself like a Hero, or to die at your Feet like a Slave, he no more than dissembles, or, if you cannot help believing him, only recollect the old Phrase, "Violent Things can never last".

Tenderness, Friendship and Constancy drest in a Simplicity of Expression, recommend themselves by a more native Elegance than violent Raptures, extravagant Praises and slavish Adoration, all which perhaps may be no more than a Repetition of the same Things said to a hundred of the Sex before.

The Motions of an honest Passion are regular and lasting; its Elegance consists in Purity, and its Transports are the result of Virtue and Reason. It never sinks a Man into imaginary Wretchedness, nor transports him out of himself, nor is there a greater Difference between any two things in Nature than between true Love and that romantic Passion which pretends to ape it.

The Whole Duty of a Woman: or. A Guide to the Female Sex
written by a Lady (1695)

... I suppose you now at Years capable of entering into the Holy State of Matrimony, Ordained at first by God in Paradise, and since not only in Sacred Writ, but highly esteemed by all the Civilized Nations. And that you may not rush upon so weighty a Thing rashly, or unadvisedly, I shall lay down some Rules and Directions, that will not only be a sure and safe Conduct, to such as are people in Stations of Eminency, but even to those of lower Degrees, so that the meanest may raise her fortune by them. For I have often observed, also cautious and prudent Management in Matters of Love, many poor Virgins are initiated into Families by Marriage, that have not barely enriched them, but given such Reputations and Credit to Vertues, that they have outshined those that a little before looked down upon them with Disdain and Contempt.

Love is the noblest Passion of the Mind, and therefore ought to be entertained as it deserves. It may be divided into two Branches, Divine and Humane, and not confounded in itself, unless abused or justled out of its Center. Or, to speak more properly, the Shadow represented for the Substance. The first Part has been, in great measure, laid down in the foregoing Discourses, and therefore I shall here only touch lightly upon it, as it occurs in the Series of the Second, my Intent being to instruct Virgins of all Degrees and Qualities in the Guidance of their Fancies, and how to distinguish them from Designs, and Counterfeit Pretences, that are too often used to ensnare their Affections.

You of the Higher Rank, who stand as it were upon Pinacles, more obvious to the Eyes of the World, must move in this great Business with the exactest Caution and Regard to your Vertues. Keep your Eyes and Tongue within Command, that though you render Civility when it is discreet so to be done, yet let them not give by Glances or Expressions, such Encouragement as may turn to Prejudice, for Men are always on the Watch, and nothing gives them greater hopes, than to see a young Lady free of Temper, forward of Talking, and willing to entertain them with her Discourse, to approve herself (as she supposes) Witty, or, as some can speak loud or be more minded, which looks as if they Beat Drums for Volunteers. But rather in all your Behaviour and Carriage in this Nice Matter, you must be extream wary, neither to provoke nor intice, till you know upon what Foundation you are, it must be such as may secure you without offending. Use no ill-bred affected Shyness, nor unseemly Roughness, but carry such Looks, as may forbid without Indecency, and oblige (as far as it is Reasonable) without Invitation, for a little Compliance in this Case, if you are not wary, may betray you into irrecoverable Mistakes. That which you may call Complaisance, will have another Construction, and make you to be thought too fond, which leaves a Blemish in lessening your Value. But above all these, beware of the Vanity of Conquest, it is a dangerous Experiment, and generally fails, being built upon so weak a Foundation, as that of too great a Confidence in ourselves, and 'tis as safe to play with Fire, as dally with Gallantry, for in this you conspire against yourself, till the Humble Gallant, who is only admitted as a Trophy assisted by the Insinuation of Love in your Breast very often becomes a Conqueror. He puts on the Stile of Victory and from an Admirer groweth into a Master, for so he may be termed from the Moment he is in Possession. The first Resolutions of stopping at Good Opinions and Esteem grow weaker by Degrees and the Charms of Courtship skillfully applied. You may be apt to think a man speaks so much Reason whilst he is commanding you, that you will have much ado to believe him in the Wrong when he is making Love to you. And when, besides the Natural Inducements our Sex has to be merciful you are bribed by well timed Flattery, then the Danger is very great. It's like a bird listening to the call of one who has laid a Snare for it.

You are to consider, That men who say Extream fine Things, many times say them most for their own Sakes; and the vain Gallant is often well pleased with his own Compliments, as he could be with the kindest Answer, and where there is not that Ostentation, you are to suspect there is a Design. For as strong Perfumes are seldom used, but where they are necessary to smother unpleasing Scents, so excessive good Words give Reason to believe they are spread to cover something, which is to gain Admittance under a Disguise; and therefore you must be upon your Guard; and consider of the Two, that Respect, in this Case, is more dangerous than Anger, by Reason it puts the best Understandings out of their Place, till second Thoughts restore them. It steals insensibly upon you, and throws down your Defences, and then it is too late to resist, for where it prevaileth too much, it groweth to a Kind of Apoplexy in the Mind, makes it giddy; and after it has seized the Understanding, it insnares you, therefore the safest Way is to treat it like a sly Enemy, and to be perpetually upon the Watch against it.

Having given these Cautions to steer an even Course in so dangerous a Sea, where so many Rocks and Sands be hid under Smooth Waters, which if not carefully avoided, will fatally shipwreck the happy Days of your Life. I come to the nearer Particulars, in which I shall set down, How you ought to receive Addresses of Love, when Generous, made by those that are deserving, and suitable to your Quality.

Let this be said as a Fundamental, That you hearken not (if you are Young, and have Parents and Friends to rely on) to any Proposals of Marriage made to you, without their Advice, divert the Address from yourself, and direct it to them, which will be the best Test imaginable for any Pretender, for if he knows himself worthy of you, he will not scruple to avow his Design to them, if he declines it, you may be satisfied he is Conscious of something he knows will not give a valuable Consideration. So that this Course will repel no Suitor, but such as it is not your interest to admit. Besides, it is most agreeable to Virgin Modesty, which should make Marriage, rather an Act of your Obedience than your Choice. For those that think their Friends too slow paced in this Affair, and seek to overgo them, give Cause to suspect they are spurred on by too warm Desires.

If their Consent be gained, and your Liking concur, you have the more warrantable Grounds to place your Affections. If upon strict Scrutiny, and deliberate Observations on the Temper, Agreeableness, Humour, Fortune, & c you find Occasion for it, yet let not the Conquest be too easie, lest it may afterwards be counted cheap. Carry yourself with an even Temper and Deportment; and, as your Love kindles, if you see Cause to let it take Fire, be sure to keep it from blazing outwardly. As much as may be, forbid all unreasonable Visits and private Retirements, that may give Suspicion. Use Civility and Modest Respect, but no Toying or Familiarity, lest your Shews of too early Fondness, flag the soaring Wings of his Passion, for what is hardest to be got, is ever most coveted, but that which is easie, is rejected. I have known many a Young lady frustrated in her Amour, in being too forward, or fantastic in her Humours. For those sober men, who know how to value you, are not only Nice, but Quick sighted to pry into your Inclinations. And he that will chuse a Wife with those Inequalities, the other will refuse her withal, understands so little what Marriage is, as promises you no great Delight with him, but if you desire to Marry Well, that is, to a Man of Sobriety and Discretion, you are obliged in Justice to bring the same qualities as he expects with you.

This may be the Occasion which keeps so many young Ladies about the Town unmarried, till they lose the Epithete of Young; Sober Men are afraid to venture upon a Humour so disagreeable to their own, lest in seeking a Help they espouse a Ruin. Let your Choice be therefore Prudent and Agreeable, as much as is reasonable in Years, that Love may increase, for if you give your hand without your Heart, for a Title or good Estate, or any other Consideration expect that marriage to be comfortless, incumbered with more Disappointments, Trouble and Vexations than you can expect Joys to flow in it, or proceed from it.

Having stated the first Degree of Love, which might reasonably have extended to all, I shall however descend a little lower, for fuller Satisfaction to you Virgins, that hold a Middle Rank and Station in the World, who, though Modesty and other Vertues ought to shine as bright in you, as in those of Quality, and unhappy Marriage is by you as much to be avoided, if you regard the Happiness of this World and the calm and peaceable Opportunities, that should bring you to the chaste Embraces of the Spiritual Bridegroom in his Kingdom of Glory. Yet you cannot expect such State and Attendance in Courtship, and therefore must not carry it with too high a Hand. However, your Caution and Vigilance ought to be no less, but be careful to avoid all pettish, peevish Niceness, as you would shun the Intrusion of unagreeable Pretenders; for that will brand you with a Haughtiness and Pride of Mind, and fright those from you that really deserve your Affections, as not fancying your Humours, though they might well enough be Enamour'd with your Person. Let your Looks then and your Demeanour be Sober and Courteous to those of Desert, and cast no Disdain or Scorn on any. If your Admirer be troublesome make it your business to shun him, especially at unreasonable Times or modestly reprove his over boldness. Dislike the Pretensions he may claim to Familiarities that seem to you unreasonable. A sober reproof sooner dashes the forward, than Words delivered in Heat of Passion, for if some find they cannot gain their Ends, yet if they see you are prone to Anger they will hardly refrain from presenting you with their Addresses. If it be but to make you injure yourself, by a vexatious Fretting in your Mind, and Uneasiness of Temper.

As your Words and Carriage are Sober, so let your Apparel be Modest and Decent, according to your Degree; for a sober Man looks on a fine Thing (that makes her Dress her chiefest Care, and thinks she is more beholden to the Taylor than Nature, for setting her off to Advantage) only as a Gaudy Idol, to whom, if he once become a Votary, he must not only sacrifice a great Part of his Fortune but all his Content; and how reasonable that Apprehension is, the Wrecks of considerable Families do too sadly attest. For when such a Man sees such an empty airy Thing sail up and down her Father's House, and looks as if she came only to make a Visit, when he findeth that her Emptiness has been extreamly busie about some very senseless Things, she eats her Breakfast Half an Hour before Dinner, to be at a greater Liberty to afflict the Company with her Discourse; and then calls for a Coach to go abroad, and trouble her Acquaintance, setting out like a Ship from the Harbour, Laden with Trifles. His Passion, tho' it was kindled, a good deal will soon expire, and he blame himself, that he could be so far mistaken, as to make his Addresses to a Gilded Butterfly, which before he had made these Observations, he had consider'd as a Phoenix, the rarest Jewel in Nature.

Be sober in your Carriage, and modest in your Apparel and Behaviour, deliver not your Speeches affectedly, as if you had studied them, yet be heedful in your Discourse, that neither any Distaste be given, by throwing out Jests, or unseasonably finding Fault, where you would not have them resented: If by Importunity you are prevailed with to go abroad with your Suitor, tho' even upon the Brims of a Contract of Marriage, do it not alone, but have one of your own Sex to be a Witness of what passes between you, lest by some Accident Matters breaking between you, this occasions scandalizing Persons to reflect on your Vertues and Good Name, and raise Suspicions in their own Fancies, that spreading, may be received as Truth by others, to the Prejudice of your Fortune. Comply not to give your Heart, before you have well weighed and advised what you are about to undertake. Let not Love blind you, but make your Choice with the eyes of your Reason, and then you are the least apt to be deceived. Consider not of Riches, and a high Birth, so much as of Vertue and Agreeableness. Those that Marry for Title and Estate, more than the Person, seldom have many happy Days in marriage, and then the main End of it is lost. For if a Marriage State be begun with Sacreligious Hypocrisy, in avowing to Love, where you Like Not, it cannot be Prosperous, and then it had better not be at all.

There are yet a lower Degree of Virgins, that have as much Claim by the Right of Creation to marriage, as any of the Highest, or Middle Rank; and these for the most Part, are such as Fortune hath reduced by Unthriftiness of their Parents to rely upon others, as Servants &c. Yet you of this Rank, by behaving yourselves modestly and discreetly, standing on your

Guard, and not easie to believe Pretensions made to you, which is many times designed upon your Chastity, without Intentions of Marriage, tho' perhaps solemnly protested, may have your Lots fall in so fair a Line, as may render you of Servants, Mistresses, and consequently Happy all your Days. Of which I might give many Instances, for where Men at first pretend or Design, and find themselves opposed by Virtue and Modesty, it insensibly ensnares them many times into a Love Passion, and compels them to admire, what before, could they have debauched, they would have detested, and change their Lawless Love into a Lawful Marriage.

Be not, however, so rash as those, who are not so Provident as to examine, how agreeable it is to their Interest, to contrive for any Thing beyond the Marriage, the Thoughts of whose future Temporal Conditions (like those of the Eternal) can find no Room amidst the foolish Rapture, but as if Love were indeed the Deity, which he is feigned to be, they depend on him for all, and take no further Care. But look before you, and consider the Charge before you enter upon it, think how to live, and live happily, And so shall your Wedding Day be a Day of Joy indeed.

THE NEW LOVER'S INSTRUCTOR
OR
WHOLE ART OF COURTSHIP

**Published under the Direction and Inspection of
Charles Freeman Esq. and Mrs Charlotte Dorrington**

THE PREFACE

It will scarcely be disputed that persons may possess good understandings, and be qualified to acquit themselves with credit in conversation, and yet be unequal to the task of

Scarcely had she so determined it, when the figure of a man on horseback drew her eyes to the window. He stopped at their gate. It was a gentleman – it was Colonel Brandon himself. Now she should hear more, and she trembled in expectation of it. But it was not Colonel Brandon; neither his air, nor his height. Were it possible, she should say it must be Edward. She looked again. He had just dismounted; she could not be mistaken – it was Edward.

delivering their sentiments upon paper, in such a manner as to do justice to the subject on which they treat.

It has been often and justly observed, that the stile of epistolary correspondence should resemble that of familiar conversation: but it must be remarked, that the conversation here meant, is not that of the vulgar and uninformed. Even those who are acquainted with the productions of polite authors, if they are unaccustomed to writing, will not be able readily to determine in what manner to express themselves; for it cannot be expected but that we must be diffident of success in every new undertaking, and despair of arriving at excellency in those arts, wherein we have not had the advantage of experience.

It is presumed, that the following collection of Letters will serve as examples for giving a clear idea of the manner in which a correspondence should be maintained on the important points of Love and Marriage. They are not the production of one pen; the greatest part of them having really passed between ladies and gentlemen, while engaged in courtship; and, therefore, it may reasonably be supposed, that the passions are expressed according to the animated dictates of nature.

There are no kinds of epistolary writing requiring so much attention as those relating to Love and Marriage: for they are generally considered as the criterion, by which a judgment is formed of the understanding; to inspire a favorable opinion of which is the most successful way of securing the conquest obtained by personal attractions.

The Letters in Verse will convince our readers, that poetical talents are happily adapted to the expression of Love; and that they may be employed to give additional force to truth, by enriching nature with all the embellishments of art.

The Conversations and Complimentary Cards are introduced, that such of our readers as, through the various avocations of life, have been denied opportunities of attending to the forms of polite expression, may, by giving a grace and polish to their language, improve rusticity into good breeding. And here it may not be improper to observe, that, though in the common occurrences of life, nothing more may be regarded than a plain declaration of our sentiments, it will be found that, in intercourses respecting Love and Marriage, unadorned truth will often fail to produce the desired effect: to ingratiate esteem, something more will be necessary than merely an endeavour to avoid exciting disgust; we must, in short, do every thing in the manner that we think will prove most agreeable to the desired object.

The Editor has now to acknowledge his obligations to those ladies and gentlemen, to whose kindness he is indebted for the best letters in the following pages; and to apologize for the few alterations he has introduced, which he conceived to be necessary, in order to give the Letters a more general turn, none of them being originally intended for the perusal of any, but the particular persons to whom they were respectively addressed.

After having long lamented, that there was no valuable work extant on the plan of the present publication, the Editor is happy in the opportunity of presenting to the public a miscellany, which cannot want a recommendation, since every page will convince the reader, that, instead of enervating or weakening, grace and elegance will give additional force to the impassioned language of the heart.

The Author

THE LOVER'S NEW GUIDE
OR, FULL
INSTRUCTIONS
CONCERNING
LOVE, COURTSHIP and MARRIAGE

LOVE LETTERS

From a Young Gentleman of Sixteen, going to the University, to a Young Lady about the Same Age, at Boarding-School, who was a Ward to the Gentleman's Father.

Dear Miss Arabella,

Being doomed to a temporary banishment from the presence of the most desirable object in life, I cannot let slip the favourable moment, which now offers, of tendering my warmest wishes for her happiness. Nurtured almost from our infancy together, the thoughts of parting fills me with more anxiety than any circumstance I ever yet experienced in life. I am persuaded, a heart, like my dear Arabella's, susceptible of the tenderest passions belonging to her sex, must share with me in the most poignant grief on this melancholy, though necessary occasion: but however distant I may be removed from the real object of my regard, her dear image will be ever present to my sight, that being too deeply impressed on my mind ever to be effaced. As on my arrival at College, the greatest part of my time will be engrossed by my studies, the only pleasure I shall be capable of enjoying, will be the happiness of gazing on my dear Girl's name, subscribed to the tenderest dictates of her heart, and transmitted to me, as a balm for a wounded mind; of this I hope she will not be sparing, as on it depends my ultimate happiness.

As the time of my departure is fixed to take place at the expiration of three days, I hope my dear Arabella will not fail of writing previous to that time; in anxious expectation of which, I remain unalterably yours,

Constantine Heartfree

The Young Lady's Answer

Sir,

Fortunately your letter arrived at a time when I stood most in need of assistance, as I must confess my mind was strangely agitated at the thoughts of parting with one, to whose family I acknowledge myself under the greatest obligations, and who himself has, by a most engaging behaviour, for a series of years past, contributed so much to my happiness.

Judge then, after this confession, whether I must not be a sharer of your grief; and, if I mistake not, my share will be the most considerable; as while you are indulging yourself in all the gaieties inseparable from a college life, the unfortunate Arabella sits melancholy at home, with no other consolation, than the reflection, that she once was happy: poor amends for the loss she now feels, in being deprived of the company of him that was most dear to her, and who perhaps, at that very moment, is enjoying the smiles of some more happy fair one.

But let me not anticipate affliction; perhaps heaven designs a more propitious fate; and that, at the expiration of this mournful trial, I may be blessed with the sight of the amiable Constantine, returned with the same unalterable affection for his poor Arabella, as when he set out to his destined exile; till which happy aera, whatever balmy comfort is in the power of mortal to give, shall be gladly administered by the forlorn

Arabella.

From the same Young Gentleman, on his Arrival at Oxford.

My Dearest Arabella,

I arrived here two days since, and now gladly embrace this opportunity of conveying to my lovely Girl the purest sentiments of an unfeigned passion. I am almost disgusted with my situation already, as, ever since my arrival, here has been one continued scene of riot and dissipation. These kind of pleasures, to me, have no charms; nor can I for a moment forget the superior excellencies of my beloved Fair one.

Oh! my Arabella, with thee I could be happy, even in the most humble station of life; but to be deprived of thee, is insupportable. How then shall I bear this long interval of happiness! I fear I shall not be able to pursue my studies: yet will I strive – strive did I say? – what! Strive to forget my Love! Oh, Heavens! It cannot be: pardon me, Arabella, the very idea distracts me. How am I bewildered in this maze of love!

If then I should drop the least unguarded expression, derogatory to the refined sentiments of my Arabella; forgive me, and impute it to the real cause. I could dwell for ever on this subject, but am this instant summoned to evening prayers, which I will gladly attend, and offer up my fervent supplications to the Deity, in behalf of my Love.

And now, my Arabella, I must conclude, with once more entreating you not to omit any opportunity of writing; as on that only depends the present happiness of your unfeigned Lover,

Constantine Heartfree.

The Young Lady's Reply

Sir,

With much pleasure I received the news of your safe arrival at Oxford. I am not at all surprised, that a mind like yours, not as yet depraved by vicious inclinations, should be disgusted at first sight of a place, which I am afraid may with more propriety be called a seminary of vice than learning.

Yet, Sir, when you become a little better acquainted, and have made some fashionable connections in this wicked place, I much question whether all your prudence and morality will be able to withstand the temptations that you are likely to meet with; and in a short time, I presume, all that rhapsody, contained in your last letter, will be entirely thrown away, and even the very name of Arabella be no more thought on, than if she had never existed.

Yet custom has rendered this sort of treatment so familiar to our sex, that we naturally look for it from the man we love, and if deceived, it gives an agreeable addition to our happiness; but this seldom proves to be the case; so true are those lines in the song, which say

> "Man was form'd to be a rover'
> Foolish woman to believe."

However, Sir, I will not condemn you without a fair trial, agreeable to the laws of the land; when if you prove your innocence to the satisfaction of the court, you shall be immediately rewarded both with the hand and heart of

Arabella.

From a Gentleman to a Lady, to whom he had long paid his Addresses, on seeing her in company with his Rival.

Madam,

The very favourable reception which my addresses ever met with from you, encouraged me to hope that your affections were not pre-engaged; that I stood first in the list of your admirers, and even sometimes I had vanity enough to think I had gained a place in your heart. The many happy hours I have spent in your company, the agreeable walks, and the little innocent liberties in which you have indulged me, all conspired to confirm my vain hopes with the most flattering ideas.

In this sweet delusion, I thought myself the happiest of mortals, and vainly imagined the time not far distant, that would crown my utmost wishes with their desired success.

What then must be my surprise, at seeing you a few nights since, in a public assembly with my declared rival? All my philosophy could not conceal my chagrin, which I plainly perceived you noticed, and that with an air of triumph at the cause. I quitted the room with disgust; ten thousand tortures racked my very soul, and in the first emotions of my grief, I determined to chastise the insolence of my rival, as I then thought it; but on recollection considered him rather as an object of envy than hatred, and should have despised the wretch who could have been blind to such superior charms.

You alone, Madam, are the object of my resentment; it is to you only I am indebted for the misery which is now entailed on me, and I am now perfectly convinced, that dear Variety is the idol of your whole sex; that every new lover meets with better success than the former, and still the last is happier than the first.

With these sentiments, Madam, I must finally take my leave; one favour only requesting, which is, when you have

"… but allow me to assure you that I have your respected mother's permission for this address. You can hardly doubt the purport of my discourse, however your natural delicacy may lead you to dissemble; my attentions have been too marked to be mistaken. Almost as soon as I entered the house I singled you out as the companion of my future life. But before I am run away with by my feelings on this subject, perhaps it will be advisable for me to state my reasons for marrying – and, moreover, for coming into Hertfordshire with the design of selecting a wife, as I certainly did."

perused these lines commit them to the flames, and thereby destroy the remembrance, as you have done the happiness of the once favoured

Charles Lovemore.

The Lady's Answer

Sir,

I received your curious epistle, and for the soul of me, could not refrain from scribbling a few lines by way of answer. What, Sir! because a lady condescends to walk out with, and indulges you in a few trifling liberties, as she does in common the other animals about her, are you to lord it over her, and assume an authority of scrutinizing into her conduct? That woman who submits to this before marriage, is likely to have a fine time of it afterwards!

Believe me, Sir, this will never be my case, and I should despise that lover who would not suffer another man to like his mistress as well as himself; indeed I think it a compliment paid to his understanding, in making her the object of his choice, which distinguished merit can attract the admiration of others.

I would advise you, Sir, to learn better in future, and as my last request, let the flame of love consume your jealousy, and then possibly you may hear farther from

Melinda Careless

From a Young Tradesman, just entered into Business, to a Gentleman's Daughter in the same Neighbourhood, with whom he had long been on terms of Friendship, but without a formal Declaration of Love.

Dear Miss,

A Fire which has been long kindling, generally proves most violent when it bursts out into a flame. This, Miss, is exactly my own case at this time: I have long conceived a passion, which has hitherto been concealed under the mask of friendship.

Conscious of my own unworthiness, I dared not avow that passion, till Fortune had placed me in a sphere of life to justify my pretensions with some degree of propriety; and that time being at length arrived, I can no longer stifle the flame which has now broke forth, and will have its way in spite of all opposition.

In plain terms, Miss, I love you to distraction: the charms of your person, added to the beauties of your mind, have rendered me your absolute slave: our sentiments are perfectly known to each other, long tried in friendship, which is the foundation of love, let us proceed to finish the superstructure by uniting our hands in the sacred bond of wedlock.

I will not presume to flatter, as I know your generous mind disdains it; therefore will not address myself to your passions, but appeal to reason only, to plead in behalf of my love. You are well acquainted with what has hitherto been my conduct in life, therefore shall only add, if I am so happy as to succeed in my wishes, the remainder of my days shall be devoted to our mutual interest, and my greatest study shall be to render myself worthy the object of my choice.

Deign then, my Charmer, to hear my humble supplications and vouchsafe to grant a kind compliance to my suit. I beg, dear Miss, an answer, for which I shall wait with as much anxiety, as a dying man does the dreadful sentence of the Physician. Accept, my dear Girl, my warmest wishes, and permit me to subscribe myself for ever your's,

Thomas Tradelove.

The Young Lady's Answer

Sir,

I received your obliging Letter. The compliments you are pleased to pay me, are far more than I merit; but gentlemen cannot avoid flattery, though they pretend to disclaim it. The task you impose on me is of such a nature, as requires much consideration before we come to a conclusion.

I remember an old adage, "Those that marry in haste, repent at leisure," which I believe is too often verified. I must confess, as a friend, you held a very high place in my esteem and also that I have spent many agreeable hours, and thought myself very happy in your acquaintance; but, Sir, love and friendship, though very nearly allied, often please most when separated; besides, Sir, there are many preliminaries to be settled, previous to a final determination.

Therefore, Sir, as your Physician, all the comfort I can now administer is, to tell you, there are hopes; after a few more visits I shall be better acquainted with your case, when you shall hear your final doom, from

Charlotte Easy.

The Young Tradesman's Reply

Angelic Fair One,

Words cannot sufficiently express the unutterable pleasure I received on perusing your kind Epistle. With extasy of Joy, I immediately cried out in the language of the Poet, "Let this auspicious day be ever sacred; no mourning, no misfortunes happen on it, let it be marked for triumphs and rejoicings, let happy lovers ever make it holy; chuse it to bless their hopes and crown their wishes. This happy day, which gives me my amiable Charlotte." For now I consider you as my own.

Perhaps you will say, I am too sanguine: it cannot be; for when a dying patient receives hopes from his physician, it is ever considered as an unfailing omen of success. You, my Love, are my Physician, and have shewn uncommon skill in restoring me to life, when almost expiring. Go on, celestial Fair One, perfect the work thou hast so well begun, and as a dying man would return unfeigned thanks to the Deity for his recovery, so do thou accompany me to the Holy Altar, and receive my sacred vows of constancy and love.

Let us not defer the happy moment, and whatever preliminaries are necessary on my part, shall be settled instantly to your utmost wishes. My love will admit of no delay, haste then my Charmer, complete my happiness, by immediately giving your hand to the impatient

Thomas Tradelove.

The Young Lady's Answer to his Second Letter.

Dear Sir,

It is in vain to conceal my passion any longer; therefore I plainly throw off all disguise, and own you are dear to me, but notwithstanding this acknowledgement, I cannot altogether approve of so much haste. My father as yet has not been made acquainted with our loves, but I believe has long suspected it, and I am persuaded, his consent may be easily obtained, as I have often heard him express the greatest regard for you, on account of the many amiable qualities you possess: therefore, Sir, you are at liberty to consult with him on the subject as soon as you think proper; and if he approves of our suit, let him determine the time and mode necessary for completing our wishes.

And now, Sir, as you have found me so compliable to your desires, I hope you will not abuse that confidence I have placed in you; but that by a strict adherence to the paths of virtue and honour, our love may increase with our years: thus mutually striving to set an example of conjugal felicity to the rising generation.

With the most affectionate regard, I must bid you a present adieu, in hopes of this being the last time of subscribing myself

Charlotte Easy.

From a Young Gentleman, one of the people called Quakers, to a Young Lady of the same Persuasion.

Esteemed Friend,

Thou mayst, perhaps, have perceived that I have long looked upon thee with eyes of love and affection. I believe thou knowest enough of me, my family, and connections, to suppose that I would not be guilty of making an offer which might be derogatory to thy character to accept.

My father is in good circumstances, and his acquirements are the produce of honest industry. His kindness to me has tempted him to bestow on me such an education, as, I hope, with the blessing of God, and the exertion of my own honest endeavours, will enable me to make a respectable figure to the world in general, and particularly to those among whom I most wish to be thought well of.

I know that thy father has not been less careful of thy education; nor less anxious that thou shouldst receive those early impressions of virtue and religion, which may influence thy future life.

On this basis, then, which I hope is a solid one, I ground my pretensions to thy favor; and if thou wilt listen to my suit, and gratify the ardent wish of my heart, to make thee happy, thou wilt confer a lasting obligation on thy

Ever faithful Friend,
Ezekiel Trusty.

The Female Quaker's Reply

Esteemed Friend

I have received thy letter, containing a plain and explicit declaration of thy love, and, on a business of this important nature, it becomes me to be equally plain and explicit. Thy cousin Jonathan has, for some weeks past, addressed me in the stile of one who wished to become my husband; and I know not how, consistently with acting honestly by him, I can give my vows to another. But for this reason, I should make no scruple to give thee the preference, though I have not hitherto perceived, to use thy own words, that thou hast looked upon me "with eyes of love and affection".

I did not know that thou hadst this partiality in my favour, or perhaps I might have treated another with more indifference, as I am not insensible of thy merits.

However, as matters are now situated, I know not how to give thee any other answer, than that I am thine assured friend.

Martha Lamb.

A second Letter from the Lover

Much respected Friend,

I consider myself as greatly obliged by the favor of thy letter, in answer to mine, which would have given me the utmost concern, had not a circumstance which hath happened within a few days past, encouraged me to hope that I yet may have the happiness of calling thee mine.

My cousin, of whom thou hast made mention is embarked for Philadelphia; nor have I any notion that he entertains any farther thoughts of seeking thee as a wife. If I had, I would not have made the present application; but would have endeavoured to resign to the fate that awaited me, however severe such a resignation might have been.

But I now hope, as the great obstacle is removed, and that as the removal appears to have been a matter of his own choice, thou wilt compassionate the case of

> Thine affectionate Friend,
> Ezekiel Trusty.

A compliant Answer to the Letter above-mentioned.

My worthy Friend,

I never entertained any doubt of the sincerity of thy heart, and the contents of thy last letter convinces me that I was not wrong in my conjecture.

The embarkation of thy cousin for America, without notice to me or my relations, and without any apology for his conduct, is a sufficient proof that the professions of his regard to me were not founded on that esteem which should be the great basis of a contract for life: and as I was prepossessed in thy favor, before I knew of thy esteem, I shall have no objection to meeting thee in the presence of our general friends, provided our immediate relations have no objection to our union. Once more I subscribe myself

> Thine assured Friend,
> Martha Lamb.

From a Young Gentleman at Boarding-school, to a Young Lady at another School in the Neighbourhood.

My dear Charmer,

The impression that your idea has made on me ever since I had the happiness of seeing you at Monsieur de Louvre's ball, is of so forcible a nature, that no time, no circumstance, can eradicate it; and I shall be the most wretched of all mortals, if some method cannot be contrived for the continuance of this correspondence, which I have prevailed on your French teacher obligingly to assist me in beginning.

Believe me, lovely Miss Clarinda, that if I am indulged in this first and most favourite wish of my heart, I shall deem myself one of the most happy, otherwise one of the most miserable of the human race.

I presume you are not unacquainted with my family or connections, and that I need not seek to give you a more undoubted proof of my honor, than by assuring you that I will, in all my actions, endeavour to approve myself worthy of the respectable line from which I am descended. I am, dear Madam, with the utmost ardor of affection, your ever devoted admirer,

Frederick Fondwell.

The Young Lady's Reply.

Sir,

I saw you at Monsieur de Louvre's ball; but I saw you with no distinction. Your figure made no impression on my heart, and I retired from the scene of pleasure with as much indifference, as if Mr Fondwell had not been present. In fact, Sir, I beheld some other gentlemen on that occasion, whose names I can recollect with more satisfaction than yours.

You say something of your family and connections. Of the first I have heard a respectable character, and I have no doubt but that the latter are of the most honorable kind.

Yet, though my heart is at present unembarrassed, I cannot think any thing of Mr Fondwell's address for many reasons, among which, the most forcible are my own youth and inexperience, and the duty I owe to that guardian who has acted to me as a second father. I cannot be unpolite enough to refuse thanking you for the distinction with which you have honored me, and am, Sir,

> Your most humble Servant
> Clarinda Poole.

A second Letter from the Young Gentleman.

Dearest of your Sex,

Unflattering as your letter is to my warmest wishes, I thank you most unfeignedly for the sincerity by which it appears to be dictated; and that it does not absolutely forbid me to hope.

Happy am I in the declaration that your heart is unembarrassed; and much happier shall I be, if it be my fate to entwine it. I will cherish the fond hope that the day may yet arrive, when I shall not be wholly indifferent to you; and in that hope, I will, if you forbid me not, make application to your guardian, as soon as I quit my present situation, which will be within a month.

The duty you mention to be due to your guardian, is, to me, one of the purest pledges of the goodness of your heart. Your youth, and inexperience, Madam, claim that you should have time to look around: and, ardent as my love is, if you will but give me leave to hope for the slightest share of your favor, after the expiration of one, two, or three years, I will gladly wait the term of probation; and in the interim I will do every thing to convince you of that warmth of affection with which I am, my dearest Clarinda,

> Unalterably yours,
> Frederick Fondwell.

The Answer

Sir,

I scarcely know how to reply to your second letter. You appear to me to be a precipitating Gentleman, in the very moment that you talk of waiting one, two, or three years. If you will apply to my guardian, I cannot help it; but remember that I shall not quit school these six months. This is all the declaration you are at present to expect, from

Your obedient servant,
Clarinda Poole.

From an Exciseman in the Country, to a Widow Gentlewoman of small Fortune.

Madam,

It is now above three years since I have been settled in this division; and I hope my conduct has been such as hath met the approbation, not only of those among whom my business lay, but of the whole neighbourhood. I will be very plain and explicit with you, Madam, as I have always been with every person with whom I have had any connections in life.

I am possessed of a little independence of sixty pounds a year; and I am told, Madam, that your fortune amounts to about the same sum. It requires no skill in calculation to prove, that two persons can live better on one hundred and twenty pounds a year, than one can on sixty.

You know that persons in my way of life are liable to be removed to distant parts at the pleasure of those who appoint them.

If you should favour my suit, for I intend this as an address, in that case I would submit it to your will, whether you would chuse to remove, or that I should resign my present employment; since my respect for you is too great, to admit of my taking any step of consequence in life without your concurrence. But even if you should disapprove of moving, it may happen, that I may be continued several years longer in my present station; and in that case, my wages would be so much in addition to our income.

As my view is serious, and the end of it marriage, I will presume to expect the favour of an answer; and I hope I need not make any apology for declaring myself,

Your most respectful admirer,
William Gage.

The Gentlewoman's Reply.

Sir,

Your civil letter demands as civil an answer. You must not accuse me of vanity, when I say that your's is not the first, or even the second address I have had on the subject of marriage, since the death of my late worthy husband; for a worthy man he was; and I should have but a bad opinion of that suitor's heart, which could not join with me in doing justice to his virtues.

Having been thus free with you, Sir, I will tell you farther, that the addresses which have been hitherto made me, have come from persons totally disagreeable to my inclinations.

With regard to my little fortune, it is at least twenty pounds a year more than you have been told: but that, even in a widow's opinion, ought to make no difference, where the man can be approved.

I have heard a very favourable account of your character, and I dare believe it is conformable to the truth. Having said thus much, it will be needless to add, that you will not be an unwelcome visitor to Sir,

Your very humble servant,
Margaret Thomas.

From a Young Gentleman of the Jewish Persuasion to the Object of his Affections.

Dear Miss Isaacs,

I have not enjoyed one hour of real repose since I had the honour of dancing with you at Mr Sylva's, on account of the marriage of his daughter with Mr Solomon Fernandez.

The idea of your agreeable person is perpetually with me; and I feel no repose, not even for a moment, either in the counting-house, on the 'change, or at the synagogue. The rise and fall of stocks has no longer any influence on my passions; nor have I any object of care, but what may arise from the reception this letter may meet with.

I have communicated the sentiments of my mind to your brother Levi, who has generously undertaken to intercede in my behalf, and to accompany you, after the duties of the Sabbath, to the White-Conduit Gardens, next Saturday, where, if you will be generous enough to attend, you will find a faithful admirer, and an ardent love in,

Dear Miss,

Your most devoted Servant,

Israel Abrahams.

The Young Lady's Answer.

Sir,

I have the favor of your letter, and if I had no inclination to consult but my own, I might possibly comply with the requisition made in the latter part of it; but you will remember that I have a mother, to whom I owe all possible duty and attachment. She has given me a liberal education, and has brought me up in the strictest principles of our religion, one material part of which is, to "honour our parents."

Now I will never so far depart from my sense of the sacredness of that obligation, as to violate the duty that I owe her.

My brother has already spoken to me in your Favor; and I will be honest enough to acknowledge, that I have no objection to Mr Abrahams on his own account. On the contrary, perhaps, I have a predilection in his favour; but if any application of the kind you seem to intend, is to be made to me, my mother's consent must be first obtained.

> I am, Sir, with great respect,
> Your most humble Servant,
> Rachael Isaacs.

The Gentleman's Reply

Dear Madam,

Oppressed by the force of my love, and the generous concession you seem to have made in my favor, I was absolutely unable to wait on your mother at your own house, lest the sight of you should have rendered me incapable of the very business which might bring me thither.

For this reason I took an opportunity of seeing her at Mr Mordecai's, in Lemon-street, Goodman's-Fields, and happy I was that I took the precaution I have mentioned: for out of your sight I was able to paint my passion in its genuine colours.

The good old lady saw its force, and has permitted me the honour of visiting you, which I will assuredly do this day, if I have not your orders to the contrary.

It is unnecessary, my dear Miss Isaacs, to mention the independence of my circumstances, with which you and your family are so well acquainted; but permit me to say, that if I had an empire, I would lay it at your feet; for I am, with unfeigned affection,

> Your most passionate admirer,
> Israel Abrahams.

The Lady's Answer

Sir,

My Mother has communicated to me what passed between her and you at Mr Mordecai's, and I have her permission to inform you that we shall drink tea this afternoon at 6 o'clock.

Your most humble Servant,
Rachael Isaacs.

From a Young Farmer, to the Daughter of another Farmer.

Dear Molly,

You well know that your father and mine are both in good circumstances, and are able to do handsome things for us, in case we should come together. It is a good two years since last Martinmas, that I first paid my respects to you, and you seem to take no more regard of me now, than you did at November fair, and faith hardly as much.

Though I be woundedly in love with you, yet I do not like to be played upon; and if Thomas Carter thinks he has a better chance than I then let him make the best on't. I have an honest heart, and wouldn't wrong any man alive, but I won't be imposed upon. So I desire you will let me have an answer by Richard, who will wait for it.

If it be that you despise me, why I can't help it, though it would give me a great deal of vexation; but if you should chuse to return love for love, I should think myself the happiest young fellow in ten parishes, and would do every thing in my power to prove myself

Your faithful lover till death,
James Barley.

The Girl's Answer.

Dear Mr James,

Your man Richard has just brought me your letter, and I could not rest a moment till I answered it. I know as well as you do, that it is above two years since you first spoke to me in a civil way, for well do I remember the day, as my poor heart can witness: but this is the first time that ever you spoke your mind out, as a body may say; and you know it was not the place of a maiden to speak first.

As to what you say of Thomas Carter, he never said a word to me but as a neighbour; and let me tell you that I could have had his betters at any time, if somebody else had not stood in the way.

As for despising you, Mr Barley, I am sure I never did; and may be, it is not quite in my power. – But no more of that. As to returning love for love, that is a bold word; but I may venture to say, that I never was unkind to any body. My mother has read these lines, and gives me leave to say that I am

Your Friend and Servant,
Mary Rose.

P.S If you have any thing more to write, my mother says, that when Richard comes this way he may leave your letter.

The Young Farmer's Second Letter

Dear Molly,

I am strangely pleased with your kind answer to my lines, and hope I wrote nothing to disoblige you. I am sure it was the farthest thing in the world from my mind if I did: but I was a little jealous of Tom Carter, because he used to look so woundedly hard upon you at church: but, dear Molly, let us think no more of these things. I have told my father how much I am in love with you, and he says he will give me the little farm at Dean-Bottom, and 400l. to stock it, when we are married. He has sent his respects to your mother, who invites us (God bless her) to dine with you next Sunday, when I hope we shall have nothing to talk about but the happy day, the licence and the ring.

Dear Molly,
Your faithful Lover,
James Barley.

From a Young Gentleman of the Law, to the Daughter of a Counsellor of Lincoln's Inn.

Madam,

I know not what it is of presumption that prompts me to the daringness of thus addressing you, to whom I am almost a stranger, on a subject the most interesting imaginable to the human heart.

Warmed with a passion which I have no language to express, I am impelled to appeal to you as the arbitress of my fate. Long, Madam, have I been acquainted with your merit, from the general voice of all who know you; but it is within a few days only that I became a slave to the superiority of your beauty. You will recollect the ball given in Bloomsbury-Square, on occasion of Mr G____'s. being called to the degree of a Serjeant at Law; and my flattering hopes tell me, it is possible that you may also recollect with what earnestness of attention, almost to rudeness, my eyes beheld you.

I would beg your pardon for the freedom with which I regarded you, if I thought it necessary to make any apology for obeying the genuine impulses of the heart; but as it is impossible to resist, so it would be idle to apologize for them.

Will you now permit me, Madam, to declare with the frankest sincerity, that I am perfectly enamoured of you, and that much of the happiness or misery of my future life will depend on your acceptance or rejection of my vows.

Above disguise, and courting no favor which I would not be solicitous to merit, I have taken the liberty of writing to your honored father, to whom I have honestly disclosed my passion. I have made him acquainted with my family and circumstances, and have enclosed the copy of the rent-roll of an estate, which will descend to me on the death of an aunt who is near ninety. Far be it from me to wish her death; but whenever that event shall happen, my circumstances will be very ample. At present they are by no means confined; and the share I have in Mr F____'s business, will enable me to maintain as a Gentlewoman, the Lady who shall honor me with her hand.

You see, Madam, I have been very explicit, as becomes the character of a gentleman. If you can persuade yourself to think favorably of my passion, I shall deem myself honored in becoming your guardian and protector for life: for I am, with the most profound regard,

> Dear Madam,
>
> > Your most devoted Admirer,
> > Charles Lyttleton.

The Lady's Reply.

Sir,

I had no sooner read your letter than I communicated it to my father, who has given me leave to say, that he will take two or three days to deliberate on your proposal, and will then write to you in a manner as explicit as he thinks your candour deserves.

In the mean time, I think myself honored by your good opinion, and am,

Sir,

Your most humble Servant,
Charlotte Coke.

From Mr Lyttleton to Miss Coke.

Dearest Madam,

I am this moment favored with a letter from your father, who has done me the honor of approving my pretensions; and permitted me to pay my addresses to you: a favor which I shall remember with gratitude to the last moment of my life: nor shall any day of that life pass over without a sincere acknowledgement of the obligation.

Permit me now, Madam, in the most ardent terms, to declare how sincerely I love you, permit me to say, that my happiness is involved in yours, and that my highest pleasure will consist in contributing to your satisfaction. When, my dear Miss Coke, shall I have the honor of declaring in person, that warmth of affection, that purity of love, with which I am, and ever must be,

Your most devoted servant,
And most faithful Admirer,
Charles Lyttleton.

Miss Coke's Answer.

Sir,

The favor of your last letter should not thus long have gone unacknowledged, but that my father has been in the country, and I was determined not to take any step of importance without his approbation: but he is now returned, and I am permitted to say, that Mr Lyttleton will always be a welcome visitor in the Old Buildings, Lincoln's Inn; and it is no pain to me to add, that when we are at the Forest, room at our table will always be found for a gentleman, of whom my father speaks in the highest terms of respect.

I have the honor to be, Sir,

Your obedient Servant,

Charlotte Coke.

Miss Theodosia Adams to Henry Brightwell, Esq.

Sir,

Departing as I do from the rules of decorum prescribed to my sex, I must trust to your good sense and politeness to excuse the seeming impropriety of my behaviour; and while I declare more than is customary for women to do, I must hope that there is one man who possesses more humanity than to affront a woman merely because she has a partiality in his favor.

I will tell you, Sir, (though blushing I tell you) that I have enjoyed little of repose since I saw you at the ball at Guildhall on Lord Mayor's Day. If you are not absolutely engaged I shall hope for the honour of seeing you in Basinghall-street, once within a week after the receipt of this letter. It is superfluous for me to mention matters of fortune, since it is well known, that mine is one of the first in the city.

I am, Sir, your most humble Servant,

Theodosia Adams.

Mr Brightwell's Answer.

Madam,

I conceive myself abundantly honored by the contents of your letter, to which I am totally at a loss how to make a proper reply. Only to seem to give a denial to a lady has something in it abhorrent to the feelings of a man of common spirit and politeness: – but what in my case can be done?

Some months ago, Madam, I might have rejoiced in the reception of such a letter as now gives me the most poignant pain. I have paid my addresses to Miss Barber, of Lothbury; my vows have been accepted; her friends have approved the intended match, and Thursday next is fixed on for the happy day.

My intended bride, with a generosity that must be pleasing to a liberal mind, begs that she may have the honor of ranking Miss Adams among the number of her friends.

I am, Madam, with a grateful sense of the favor you intended me,

Your most obliged and devoted servant,
Henry Brightwell.

An honest Tar's Farewell to his Sweetheart, previous to his sailing on a secret Expedition.

Dear Susan,

With great reluctance I must now bid you a present farewell: my country calls, and with pleasure I obey, regretting nothing but the absence of my dear girl. Her presence would inspire me with courage to face an host of foes; but as that happiness is denied me, the only consolation left is the hopes of a speedy return, crowned with laurels of victory, and loaded with the spoils of the enemy. The very idea of such a meeting with my dear Susan, after a painful absence, fills me with inexpressible joy. How eagerly then shall I embrace the happy moment, when fortune shall not only give me an opportunity of beholding all that is dear to me on earth, but at the same time shall enable me to tender her my future services through life.

Thus, my dear Susan, if this sweet idea should be realized, of which I flatter myself there is little doubt, shall we pass the remainder of our lives in a state of perfect joy and tranquility, uninterrupted with the anxiety annexed to a seafaring life. One thing only, my dear girl, permit me to mention, which is, that notwithstanding the inexpressible pleasure which must arise from a domestic life, with so amiable a partner, yet if at any future period my presence shall be deemed necessary to assist in chastising the insolence of our insidious foes, every other consideration, however endearing, must give place to the love and duty I owe to my king and country.

With these sentiments I am persuaded my dear Susan will agree; as a woman will never be secure in the affection of a man, who is base enough to desert his country in time of danger.

And now, my dear Susan, I must once more bid you adieu. Our sails are spread, and the whole ship's crew seem impatient to be gone: so eagerly does a true English seaman wish for an opportunity of displaying his native courage against every hostile invader. Fired with the same laudable ambition, excuse me from saying more at this time, than that I am for ever yours,

Ben Stoutoak.

P.S. Let me hear from you as soon as possible, and direct for me on board the Invulnerable at Plymouth; as we may yet be some days in harbour.

The Young Woman's Answer

Dear Ben,

With great grief I heard the news of your departure: where you are bound, or whether I shall ever see you again, God knows; and to him I shall offer up my daily prayers for your safety and preservation. Oh Ben! did you but know what I suffer at this time, indeed you would pity me, but why should I repine when you are called upon to revenge your country's wrongs, and what are the sufferings of an individual compared to those of a whole nation? Yet, though I cannot but regret your absence, I shall endeavour to console myself as much as possible with the hopes that the time will shortly arrive, when I shall behold you returning in triumph, crowned with victorious honours: till which happy day I must now bid you a sad farewell, and in anxious expectation of which, I remain unalterably yours,

Susan Truelove.

A Second Letter from the same honest Seaman on his return to England, after having made a very prosperous and victorious Voyage.

Dear Susan,

I have now the pleasure of informing you, that our ship arrived safe at Spithead last night; that after having given the French a hearty drubbing, I am returned sound wind and limb, and wish for nothing but the sight of my dear Susan, which I hope will be in a few days, as I expect to be ordered to London, as a guard to the immense treasure which we have taken from the enemy.

After cruising some time in the Bay, during which time we took several small prizes, we joined the grand fleet off Cape Finisterre; a few days after which, we met with the combined fleets of France and Spain, with a very large convoy of rich merchantmen homeward bound. Our admiral immediately gave the signal for a general engagement, which was instantly obeyed, and continued with great bravery on all sides, for the space of six hours, without any material difference, except from the loss of men, which was very considerable on the side of the enemy, as our shot did amazing execution. Night coming on we were obliged to desist, though much against the inclinations of our brave seamen, who could hardly be prevailed on by their officers to wait till day-light for a renewal of the attack.

Such a good look-out was kept during the night, that few, if any, of the merchantmen escaped.

No sooner day-light appeared, than we again began the attack with redoubled vigor, which they returned with much courage, but at length were obliged to submit to the superior power of Old England, which, in spite of all opposition, will ever remain master of the sea. One of the French-men maintained a running fight with our ship for six glasses; but we pouring into her a broadside betwixt wind and water, Monsieur was obliged to strike his flag to our brave English boys. Upon the whole, we have taken six of their large ships, and about twenty merchantmen, which we have conducted in triumph to Old England.

As in all probability this action, my dear Susan, will put an end to the war, I shall shortly have an opportunity of enjoying the treasure I have acquired at the hazard of my life, with her for whose sake only life was worth preserving; when that happy day arrives, I hope to convince the British Fair, that the heart of a true seaman is a prize of no inconsiderable value, and well worth attaining.

> As I hope to be with my dear girl in a few days,
> shall now conclude, with assuring her that
> I remain her constant lover,
> Ben Stoutoak.

From a Linen-Draper's Apprentice to a Silk-Mercer's Daughter.

Dear Miss,

The term of my apprenticeship being almost expired, the latter part of which indeed has passed almost imperceptibly, owing to the happiness I have received from your agreeable conversation, and that engaging sprightliness of disposition for which you are so justly distinguished from the generality of your sex, whose inanimate souls are scarce capable of kindling a spark of desire, while the charms of your person, joined with the natural vivacity you possess, never fail to create a flame in the heart of every one who approaches you. To you, then, Miss, I acknowledge myself under the greatest obligations, and as I would not wish to be thought ungrateful, permit me to make some kind of return for the many favors received. If then a heart wholly unattached to any one but yourself, and incapable of ever altering, be deemed worthy of your acceptance, I shall think myself happy in bestowing it; perfectly convinced, that I can never meet with an object so truly deserving. With these sentiments, Miss, permit me to add, that as I have hitherto found so much pleasure in bondage, I am encouraged to pursue it, and am resolved, with your permission, to suffer myself to be again put in chains, and hope for a much longer term of years than before. Shall think myself happy, Miss, in hearing your sentiments on this subject, which I beg you will convey in a line as soon as possible, to your most passionate admirer,

William Draper.

The Young Lady's Answer.

Sir,

Permit me in the first place to acknowledge my obligations for the many compliments you are pleased to pay to my person and my accomplishments, which I am sensible are far more than they deserve; but Gentlemen will flatter. The task you impose on me, is of such a nature, that it requires much more experience in life, than I have yet had, to be able to perform it. And I would advise you, Sir, not to be too hasty; as, however fond you may be of bondage at present, perhaps when you have enjoyed a little of the sweets of liberty, all these fine sentiments may be thrown away and forgotten. Therefore, Sir, as you have experienced the one, give the other a fair trial also; and then, if you are resolved to wear the chains, no doubt but you may meet with many ladies to enslave you, more deserving than

Jenny Lutestring.

The Young Linen-Draper's Reply

Dear Miss,

The receipt of your letter gave me much satisfaction, as it was a pleasure I never before experienced; but must confess, on perusing the contents, I found myself much chagrined and disappointed, as I vainly imagined what I had wrote, and conscientiously thought to be the purest dictates of my heart, would be implicitly believed so by every one else; but am now convinced of my error, and acknowledge myself indebted to you only for the discovery; but, notwithstanding this confession, I hope to convince you by my perseverance, that I still continue to prefer, and ever shall, a life of bondage with you, to all the ideal charms of liberty. Permit me then, thou idol of my soul, to repeat in the most tender and pure manner, my most ardent professions of esteem and love, that there is no other object on earth that appears to me desirable, but yourself; and that however fortune may please to smile on me through life, my happiness will be incomplete, till joined with you in the sacred bands of wedlock.

Deign then, my charmer, to grant a favorable answer to my petition, relieve me from the anxiety I now feel, and restore me to happiness by accepting both the hand and heart of,

William Draper.

The Young Lady's Answer.

Sir,

I am really at a loss how to answer your last letter. Impressed with a sense of gratitude on the one hand for the very favorable opinion you seem to entertain of me; yet, on the other side, I dread giving my assent to your generous offers, not through any dislike to your person, morals, or connections, but only through fear that you should hereafter repent your bargain. However, Sir, permit me to repeat my former advice, of not being too hasty: time perhaps may produce a change in us both: and who knows but she, who now appears the most cold and insensible to the refined passion of Love, may in a short time be most forward to promote a passion she now treats with so much indifference?

Despair not then, while there are hopes still left, of obtaining her you are pleased to deem the object of your wishes, in the person of

Jenny Lutestring.

To a Lady, who had approved the Addresses of the Writer.

Madam,

Your condescension in allowing me to write to you during your stay at Brighthelmstone has laid me under an obligation that I shall ever gratefully acknowledge. But though making one favor the foundation of asking another, may have the appearance of want of generosity, I cannot refrain from earnestly entreating that you will occasionally honor me with a few lines in reply.

Perhaps you may say, that a necessary regard to punctilios will not admit of your compliance; but permit me to observe, that there can be no reasonable ground for concealing the nature of our intercourse from the knowledge of the world, my pretensions being honorable, and not unfavourably received, either by yourself or your friends; a correspondence may therefore be maintained without any breach of propriety.

Believe me, Madam, you were mistaken in supposing that I should recover my tranquility in a short time after your departure. Every moment brings additional sorrow; and it is in vain that I exert my endeavours to divert my mind from the only object that it can contemplate with delight.

While you are happy in the society of agreeable friends, and partaking of those elegant amusements which are usual at Brighthelmstone at this season of the year, I am labouring under all the distress that is possible for a human heart to experience. Where the greatest perfections of the mind are added to the most enchanting beauty, a single glance is sufficient to warm the cold blood of an anchorite into a quicker current. Can I then be free from alarms, while you are surrounded by persons of fashion, among whom there are many, that it would argue extreme folly were I to dispute with for superiority, in those points by which female regard is supposed to be attracted?

However, if you will please to favour me with a letter, the pleasing hope will revive, that I hold some place in your esteem; but alas! I am terribly apprehensive that balls, card-assemblies, and other amusements that unite to fill up the circle of pleasure, exclude from your mind all recollection of,

Madam,

Your most faithful and devoted Admirer,
William Tremble.

The Answer

Sir,

After a long debate with myself, I at length came to a resolution of complying with your request; though it would perhaps have been more prudent to decline it. I am sorry you have given me reason to accuse you of hypocrisy, which is a vice of so hateful a nature, that the person who is guilty of it seldom fails to forfeit the esteem of those by whom it is detected. You insinuate, that you are apprehensive of being supplanted by a rival; and therefore you must entertain a most unworthy opinion of me, or have spoken a language foreign to your heart. After having accepted your overtures of marriage, can it be supposed that I would countenance those of another? If you believed me capable of such a conduct, you could not entertain the affection you profess.

The rhapsody about the perfections of the mind, &c. is certainly inconsistent with that part of your letter, where you represent me as a poor weak creature, in most violent danger of being seduced into the paths of indiscretion, by the allurements that are supposed to attract female regard. For my part, I know not what are stronger attractives to female regard, than good sense, probity, and honor; nor what characters we look upon with more disgust than those, which, in compliance with an absurd prejudice, insult us by unworthy suspicions.

It is true, I have been at balls, card-assemblies, the theatre, and, in short, have partaken of every amusement this place affords; and, what may appear very extraordinary to you, have found that my conduct has, in no instance, merited reproach.

Indeed, I am of opinion, that innocent recreations are necessary for promoting and preserving health; and that is an object we cannot neglect, without being guilty of ingratitude to the Author of our being. Such entertainments then, as tend to exhilarate the spirits, without having any dangerous effects upon the morals, may be enjoyed with advantage, provided we do not suffer them to obtain so great an ascendancy over our minds as to detach us from the more important duties of life. However, I will not pursue this serious strain, but proceed to an account of what I have seen during my stay in this part of the country.

Brighthelmsone stands on an eminence, commanding a view of the sea, and a finely variegated country to a great extent. On that part of the Steyne adjoining to the town, is a fine lawn, where the company walk morning and evening, while they are entertained by a good band of music supported by public subscription; this is a spot perhaps the most delightful in the kingdom. The road leading hence towards Steyning, affords a prospect astonishingly grand; here appears a range of hills, projecting in the boldest manner; and we behold the wilds of Kent and Sussex, and many miles of rich inclosure, seemingly in another region, so surprising is the height of the hills.

The majority of the inhabitants of this place are fisherman; and when the women are not engaged in household business, they employ themselves in repairing the nets belonging to the men; and thus employed, they really afford a very pleasant sight, being particularly neat in their appearance, and seemingly of vivacious and affable dispositions.

This town has a good market, constantly supplied with great plenty of the best provisions, but the mutton deserves particular mention; for being fed on the Downs, which afford a fine pasture, intermingled with diverse sorts of aromatic herbs, it receives a flavor more delicious than that of the sheep produced in any other part of England.

I remember to have somewhere read, that the remains of Druidical altars abound in the neighbourhood of Brighthelmstone; but I have not been able to learn where any of these vestiges of antiquity are to be seen.

I shall now conclude, with observing, that though I cannot answer for what change of disposition a few weeks may produce, yet I will not wilfully cause you any unhappiness, while I remain

Fanny Firm.

The Gentleman's Second Letter

Indeed, my dear Madam, you letter has relieved me from a state of the most insupportable affliction. I will candidly acknowledge that I had apprehensions exceedingly alarming: but why should those doubts (allowing them to have no just foundation) give rise to your displeasure? Had you made a declaration in my favor, or intimated a warm partiality towards me, I could not have made use of such expressions as those contained in my former letter, without offering you a direct affront. But fearing you might have permitted my addresses, rather in compliance to the advice of your friends, than from your own judgment, I could not but be exceedingly anxious, lest so inestimable a jewel should become the prize of some other of your numerous admirers. However, all the clouds that obscured my view to happiness are now dispersed. The concluding lines of your letter convey a meaning, that I could not say I was at a loss to interpret, without being guilty of the most palpable affectation. I have learnt that you mean to set out for London tomorrow, and I must entreat, that you will permit me to wait upon you the following day, to declare with how much veneration I am,

> Dear Madam,
>> Your ever obliged and devoted
>> William Tremble.

From a Young Tradesman to a Neighbour's Daughter, soliciting her in Marriage.

Madam,

You may be surprised that I should take this method of declaring my sentiments, when the friendly terms on which I live with your nearest relations, give me such frequent opportunities of engaging you in a particular conversation. The truth, in short, is, that I have many times determined to disclose my mind, but when at the point of entering upon the subject, my resolution has constantly deserted me. Such is the influence of your charms, that the moment you appear, all my faculties are absorbed in admiration; my frame is shook with an universal tremor; and by endeavouring to conceal the agitation of my spirits, I but add to my confusion, and become still more ridiculous.

Some lovers would improve the advantage of having free access to an admired object; but it is my misfortune to want that share of confidence which would contribute to my peace of mind, and, perhaps, facilitate the attainment of my desires.

If you have any previous engagement, or an unconquerable objection to my person, I will immediately decline all pretensions to your favor: but because I affect not a fashionable gallantry, let me entreat you not to suppose my passion the less fervent or sincere.

... captivated by youth and beauty, and that appearance of good humour, which youth and beauty generally give, [Mr Bennet] had married a woman whose weak understanding and illiberal mind had, very early in their marriage, put an end to all real affection for her. Respect, esteem, and confidence had vanished for ever; and all his views of domestic happiness were overthrown. But Mr Bennet was not of a disposition to seek comfort, for the disappointment which his own imprudence had brought on, in any of those pleasures which too often console the unfortunate for their folly or their vice. He was fond of the country and of books; and from these tastes had arisen his principal enjoyments.

112

If I am so happy as to obtain your permission, I will submit my proposals to the consideration of your friends, and endeavour to obtain their concurrence to our union; and I shall now conclude with a solemn promise, that, to contribute towards your happiness shall ever be the principal care of him who now presumes to subscribe himself,

Madam,

Your most passionate and respectful Admirer,
Frederick Nicholls.

The Lady in Reply to the above.

Sir,

I received your letter, and was at no loss to determine in what manner I should reply. I must confess myself obliged by the favorable opinion you entertain of me, and at the same time assure you, that the proposals you make cannot possibly be accepted, I do not say this, because I am already under engagements of the nature you allude to, but because a part of your conduct threatens all that can prove subversive of domestic happiness. But, Sir, I mean to be plain, that we may understand each other, without continuing the correspondence. The reprehensible part of your conduct then, is an attachment to gaming: your propensity to this scandalous and destructive practice, was not known in our family till within these few weeks; within which time you cannot but have observed, that my father and brother have taken unusual pains to engage you to spend your evenings at our house; and to this they were induced by a desire of detaching you from your dissolute companions: but they have now relinquished the hopes of succeeding; for they have with much concern observed, that after taking leave of our family you have, for some time past, gone to a neighbouring tavern, which is notoriously a receptacle for gamblers, sharpers, and cheats of every denomination; and I fear, that the imprudent conduct I am speaking of has become so habitual, that their influence will be insufficient to convince you of the necessity of a reformation.

I beg, Sir, you will not make a second application, and assure you that my resolution is unalterable. Perhaps, I have expressed myself with too much freedom: if you think so, I beg you will attribute it to my candor, and deem it as proceeding from a desire of assigning a competent reason for rejecting your proposal. I am, Sir,

Your obliged humble Servant,
Maria Selkirk.

The Lover refutes the Suspicion of his being addicted to the Vice of Gambling.

Dear Madam,

Be assured, I am perfectly innocent of what is alleged against me: but I will immediately proceed to an explanation. It is true, that I have of late been many times at the tavern you mention: but when you learn on what motive, you will, I am confident, esteem me deserving of commendation rather than censure.

You are not ignorant, Madam, that a young gentleman, the son of one of my foreign correspondents, has resided some weeks at my house. This youth, though possessed of an excellent heart, has some considerable foibles, one of which is, a fondness for scenes of gaiety and dissipation. After returning from the theatres, or other places of public amusement, I fortunately discovered that it was his constant practice, to join a set of abandoned scoundrels, with whom he spent the greatest part of the night at the billiard-table. I expostulated with him on the dangerous connections he had formed, but found him so strongly prepossessed in favor of his new companions that all the arguments I was able to enforce, were not strong enough to convince him of their iniquitous practices. I communicated the matter to a friend, and he proposed accompanying me to the tavern in the evening. There is reason to suppose, my presence restrained our young Bavarian from hazarding any considerable sums. We several times repeated our visits, but, from our entire ignorance of the game, were unable to detect the villainy which we suspected, at length, the sharpers applied to my friend, to become an accomplice in their scheme, he having, by an ingenious stratagem, caused them to mistake his person for that of a famous gambler, whom, he learnt, they were unacquainted with, by listening to their private conversation. This, and other circumstances, enabled us to detect them in the actual practice of a number of infamous artifices for robbing the inexperienced youth of a very large sum, which in the openness of his heart he had informed them, was all that remained of what his father had allowed for his support, during a residence of three years in this country: and it was only a few hours before the receipt of your letter, that the whole fraternity were apprehended and taken before a magistrate, who compelled them to refund near five hundred pounds.

Having thus removed the cause of her objection, I cannot but flatter myself in the pleasing hopes of being admitted to the honor of visiting my dear Maria in the character of a lover. I have already declared my sentiments to your father, and obviated the prejudices he had conceived in consequence of my attendance at the tavern. He does not disapprove my proposal; but says, he has so entire a confidence in your discretion, that he will attempt to put no constraint upon your will; and your brother has kindly promised to intercede with you on my behalf. On this encouragement, I mean to take the liberty, with your permission, of waiting upon you at seven o'clock to-morrow evening, and in the mean time permit me to say, that I am, with unalterable affection,

Madam, your most obedient servant,
Frederick Nicholls.

The Young Lady's Answer.

Sir,

My father has permitted me to say, that I may accept your visits; in consequence of which, I shall be glad to see you to-morrow evening.

I am, Sir, your very humble Servant,
Maria Selkirk.

From a Young Tradesman who had much impoverished himself through Extravagance, to a rich Farmer's Daughter in Yorkshire.

Madam,

When at last York meeting, I craved the honor of your hand at the assembly, which, I flatter myself, you cannot have forgot. The favor I asked, you readily granted with the most obliging condescension, and I then enjoyed the happiness of having you for my partner during the whole evening. The dances being ended, you suffered me to wait on you home, during which time I made you acquainted with my name, business, and connections in life, to which I had the vanity to think you seemed to listen with some degree of attention and approbation. At our parting, you granted me permission to visit you the ensuing day, which liberty I was unhappily deprived of, by receiving the news, that very evening, of the death of a very near relation in London. This unfortunate event rendered my immediate presence absolutely necessary, and in consequence of which I set out very early the next morning for town.

Believe me, Madam, I had a most melancholy journey, as the business I was going on was, in itself, of a very disagreeable nature; but what was ten thousand times worse, it deprived me of the opportunity of seeing the dearest object of my wishes, and for whom I had conceived the most tender passion. Judge then, Madam, the anxiety of mind I must undergo, at being so suddenly torn from every thing I held dear and valuable, and at the same time knew not what unfavorable construction might be put on my abrupt departure, you not being apprized of the real cause. I determined then, on my arrival in London, to embrace the earliest opportunity of supplicating a pardon, which I flatter myself, now you are made acquainted with the case, you will not scruple to grant.

I hope, ere long, to have the happiness of seeing you again at York, and shall think every moment an age, till I am once more blessed with a sight of your adorable person.

In the mean time, Madam, suffer me to make a tender of my future services, by offering you a heart wholly devoted to yourself, and incapable of deceit. If a passion of the purest and most exalted nature, be worthy your regard, I think I may justly claim some share in your esteem.

Permit me then to hope, if some one more happy than myself has not already engaged your affections, (which gracious heaven forbid!) that my utmost wishes will be crowned with their desired success; and my life and fortune shall be wholly devoted to the happiness of yours. Suffer me then to hope for your kind compliance, and relieve me from the most torturing suspense, by the favor of a few lines of approbation; in anxious expectation of which, I remain

Your devoted Slave and Admirer,
Christopher Careless.

The Young Lady's Reply.

Sir,

With much surprise, I received your letter, and often debated with myself whether it would be prudent in me to answer it. As to my behaviour at the assembly, in suffering myself to become your partner in a dance, it is nothing more than what is customary in the place, and might have happened to any indifferent person as well as yourself; therefore I can see no right you have to claim any liberties on that account.

As to your pretended passion, I conceive it to be nothing more than words of course, and what might naturally be expected from any gentleman in a similar situation; indeed, I think no woman can be weak enough to believe any gentleman could be so deeply smitten at first sight, and should rather imagine he had something more to interest him in the pursuit than mere love; and, Sir, as I would wish to be ingenuous with you, I must confess I have received some intimation of your design: in plain terms, Sir, it has been whispered through the City of York, by some persons who saw you at the assembly, and pretended to be well acquainted with your real situation in life; that your father, a few years since, left you possessed of a very considerable fortune, and also the business by which he had acquired it; since which time, you had led a most dissolute life, and thus by practising all the fashionable vices of London, have reduced your fortune to a very low ebb, and that unless you can retrieve yourself by marriage, a bankruptcy is inevitable.

These, Sir, are the charges exhibited against you, and as you intimate a design of re-visiting me at York, I must beg leave to decline the intended honor, till such time as the above charges are refuted, I am, Sir,

Your well-wisher, and humble Servant,

Margaret Cautious.

The Young Tradesman's Reply

Madam,

The receipt of your letter, with the charges therein contained against me, I now consider as the happiest event in my life, as it has brought me to a state of reason, to which before I was an utter stranger. I have long been in a lethargy, from which, by your kindness, I am now perfectly awaked, and can justly say with the Poet, "Thro' all the roving pleasures of my youth, where nights and days seemed all consumed in joy; where the false face of luxury displayed such charms as might have shaken the most holy hermit, and made him totter at his altar, I never knew one moment's peace like this."

To you, Madam, I acknowledge myself indebted for this wonderful change. To you then will I appeal as judge in my behalf, and after a candid hearing, will submit myself to any sentence you shall think proper to inflict.

In the first place, Madam, I confess, that being of a volatile disposition, and hurried on by the passions of youth, I have suffered myself to be too often led into the fashionable follies and extravagancies with which this place abounds; but that I never yet quitted the paths of honor. That in consequence of my irregular mode of living, I must also confess, that my fortune is considerably diminished, but so distant from a bankruptcy, that after discharging all my debts, I shall have a sufficiency left to maintain a genteel independency.

The last accusation is, that my fortune being greatly reduced, I had no other alternative, than retrieving it by marriage. This charge I have before refuted, by proving that my affairs were not in so alarming a situation as was generally imagined; but I will not absolutely deny that I ever entertained a thought of that nature; on the contrary, I conceived it to be a very eligible plan, and have often mentioned it as such, but never attempted to put it into execution.

With regard to yourself, Madam, I protest in the most solemn manner, that I never was actuated by any other motive than pure and disinterested love.

On your first entering the assembly room, I was struck with the charms of your person, and determined from that moment to make you an offer of my heart. During the course of the evening, I was convinced that the mental qualities you possessed were equal to the beauty of your person, which, added to a most enlivening conversation, an infinite fund of wit, and a most engaging disposition, all conspired to complete the conquest.

Thus, Madam, as I have given a true state of the case, I hope I shall receive my pardon, signed by your delicate hand, by the return of the post, after which I may once more be permitted to visit York, and be blessed with the sight of my adored Fair One.

Permit me, dear Madam, to subscribe myself with the utmost sincerity, your faithful Lover,

Christopher Careless.

The Lady's Reply.

Sir,

I cannot but acknowledge, that in your last letter there breathes an air of sincerity, which seems to carry conviction with it, and which leads me to hope, that your boasted reformation is built on a solid foundation, and able to withstand the vast stream of fashionable dissipation, with which it is environed. How happy then shall I think myself, in being instrumental to so great a change; at the same time that I rejoice with you on your escaping the horrid precipice, from which you was in imminent danger of plunging into irretrievable ruin! I cannot but lament the depravity of human nature, that the vices and follies of our fellow-creatures, instead of exciting pity, are artfully related in a private assembly, and thence propagated throughout every polite circle in town, with the most exaggerating circumstances; so that a gentleman, who by a run of ill-luck happens to lose a few guineas at a card or billiard table, and the story becoming once known, stands a chance of being accused of mortgaging his estates, being reduced to poverty, turning fortune-hunter, which scheme miscarrying, goes upon the highway, and at last suffers an ignominious death as a felon; and all this perhaps proceeds from no other cause, than a sudden disappearance having furnished these reputation-murderers with matter sufficient to exercise their fertile imaginations, and gratify their envious dispositions with the most malicious slander. This, Sir, might probably have been your case, had you not received timely notice, and thereby vindicated your reputation and honor, which I think you have done so much to the credit of yourself and friends, that if you persevere in your design of re-visiting York, you may be assured of a hearty welcome, from

Margaret Cautious.

From a Young Gentleman of Fortune, to a reputable Trademan's Daughter, persuading her to elope from her Parents, who had refused their Consent to her Marriage with the Young Gentleman, of whom she was passionately fond, and was endeavouring to force her to marry the son of a neighbouring Tradesman, whom she detested.

Dear Miss,

It is impossible for words to describe the tortures that I daily undergo, on being deprived of the sight of the loveliest of her sex. Oh! my dear Fanny, did you but know the miserable state of a despairing lover, surely you could not hesitate one moment, but fly into the arms of him whose life is entirely devoted to love and you.

Perhaps, at this very moment, my dearest girl may be forced for ever from my sight, and obliged, by the cruelty of an unrelenting parent, to give her hand to my most detested rival. Dreadful idea! If that fatal event has not already happened, let me conjure my amiable girl, with all the tenderest eloquence of a most passionate admirer, to relieve me from this most dreadful suspense, by flying instantly from impending ruin; and rely on the protection of him who is ready to sacrifice his life for her sake.

I flatter myself, my dear, that you are already convinced my views are wholly disinterested, as fortune has amply provided for our future support: then why should we waste a moment of our time, by deferring a happy union of souls so perfectly formed for each other? The plan, my dear, I have adopted for your deliverance and my happiness, is of such a nature as cannot fail of success, and however unkind your father may at present appear, I have no doubt but a little time will convince him of his error, and remove the prejudices he has unhappily conceived against me. Grant then, my love, a favorable answer to my wishes, and thereby perfect the happiness of

Your most faithful Admirer,
Valentine Truelove.

The Lady's Answer

Sir,

Notwithstanding I acknowledge the very favorable opinion I entertain of you, and what is still more, that you are the only man with whom I could be happy; yet, Sir, the obligations I am under to my parents, for their tender care of me from my infancy to the present time, are so many, and of such a nature, that nothing ever shall induce me to swerve from my duty, though at the expence of my own happiness. My father, cruel as I now think him, in endeavouring to force my hand to the man I most abhor, will, I hope, in time relent, and pity his unhappy daughter.

As, Sir, I have now declared my determined resolution, never to make my parents unhappy by a neglect of the duty I owe them, consequently I cannot by any means consent to your scheme of elopement; therefore must entreat you not to say any more on that subject; but as I am at present denied the pleasure of seeing you, I hope you will embrace every opportunity that offers of writing, and which you may depend will not be neglected on my side.

This is the only consolation I can possibly expect or enjoy in my unhappy situation, and even this must be managed with the utmost prudence and caution; as, should a letter once be intercepted, it would probably not only increase my present misery, by a closer confinement, but utterly prevent our future correspondence.

And now, Sir, let me prevail on you to reconcile yourself to your present situation, indulging yourself with the pleasing hopes of the time coming, when we shall yet be happy. Of this you may be assured, that though I never will be instrumental to my parents unhappiness, by marrying, contrary to their inclination, the man they shall disapprove; yet, on the other hand, no power on earth shall ever force me to a union with the man I detest; that I will ever remain a stranger to the happiness of a married state, or enjoy the object of my choice; and finally, that no man but yourself shall ever receive the hand or heart of

Fanny Pleasant

From a Young Gentleman, on a Quarrel which had happened with a Lady to whom he had long paid his Addresses.

Madam,

After the long and agreeable intimacy which had subsisted between us, how my unlucky stars created a breach last night I know not; but when I awaked this morning, and reflected on the transactions of the preceding evening, how was I shocked at the very idea of offending the dear girl I adore!

Stung with the keenest remorse for my past offences, I determined instantly to expiate my fault by a candid confession of it, and a sincere repentance.

Accept then, dear Madam, this confession as an atonement for the enormity of my crimes, and admit the future zeal and devotion at the shrine of your beauty to obtain my pardon; so shall I hope hereafter to be made partaker of such joys as the warmest language but faintly can express.

Deign then, thou Goddess of my idolatry, to hear my earnest prayers and supplications, and relieve me from the excruciating pangs I now feel, by absolving all past offences, and thereby restoring to happiness the now miserable

Timothy Telltruth.

The Lady's Reply.

Sir,

As the only method to obtain forgiveness for our sins, is by an open confession and true repentance, I know not how far I might be led to forgive, could I believe your repentance sincere; but, Sir, I much fear, that you finding forgiveness so easily obtained, might shortly be tempted to fall into the same errors again, and thereby become ruined irretrievably.

Therefore, Sir, as I have a sort of regard for you still left, I think it most prudent to defer granting an absolute pardon 'till your future behaviour has proclaimed you worthy of it. If then you think my forgiveness worth procuring, you will instantly set about a reformation, which, once perfected, will be sure to obtain a general pardon, and total oblivion for all past offences committed against

Sabina Lofty.

From a Young Gentleman of Fortune, to an amiable Young Widow in the same Neighbourhood, who, a short time since, had been released from a Life of Misery, by the Death of a most difficult and abandoned Husband.

Madam,

From my connections in the neighbourhood of your residence, you cannot suppose me quite ignorant of the many amiable

In as short a time as Mr Collins's long speeches would allow,
everything was settled between them to the satisfaction of both;
and as they entered the house, he earnestly entreated her to name
the day that was to make him the happiest of men; and though
such a solicitation must be waived for the present, the lady felt no
inclination to trifle with his happiness. The stupidity with which he
was favoured by nature must guard his courtship from any charm
that could make a woman wish for its continuance; and Miss Lucas,
who accepted him solely for the pure and disinterested desire of an
establishment, cared not how soon that establishment were gained.

virtues you possess, nor of the charms of your person. Those charms, Madam, have attracted my admiration a thousand times, and I have cursed the wretch who was possessed of such a jewel without knowing the value of it: but Heaven has at length thought fit to remove him, and left you, the brightest gem in the creation, as a blessing to some more deserving object.

Permit me, Madam, with the utmost respect, to subscribe my name in the list of your admirers, and should I be so happy as to be thought an object worthy of your regard, I should deem myself the happiest of mortals.

Elate with such a heavenly prospect, suffer me, Madam, to tender you a heart which has long languished for you, who are the sole object of my love. Deign then to pity your devoted slave, and grant him the privilege of visiting your adored person; when, if I do not convince you of the purity of my passion, discard me for ever from your sight, and thereby render me the most miserable of the human race.

In anxious suspence, I wait to receive my doom from your fair hand; till when, suffer me to subscribe myself,

Your most passionate Admirer,
D. Trusty.

CONVERSATIONS
On the Subjects of
LOVE AND MARRIAGE.

Conversation the First.
Between a Lady of Fortune and her Son.

Lady. You know, Frederic, with what fondness I have regarded you during your childhood and youth; what attention I have paid to your education; and how truly I have considered your interest as the dearest part of my own.

Son. I am not insensible, Madam, to the kindness you have shewn me from my birth to the present hour;-but to what purpose does this observation tend?

Lady. I need not tell you that the death of your father was such a drawback on the happiness of my life, as no subsequent event has been able to make good; and your good sense will inform you, that if I have any tolerable chance of comfort for the remainder of my days, it must result from the seeing you happy.

Son. Once more, Madam, I must beg you will inform me what you have in view; – I have not been accustomed to disobey your commands.

Lady. Marriage, my dear Frederic, is one of the first and most important concerns of human life; – but, before I proceed, may I hope that your heart is disengaged?

Son. The question is a sudden one, Madam; but suppose that it were not?

Lady. Then I should be sorry that I had said a word on the subject; for I would no more wish to control your inclinations, than I would that my own should submit to the unreasonable will of another.

Son. You are ever generous, Madam, – let me beg that you would speak your mind with freedom.

Lady. Miss Silvester of Harley Place is---

Son. A most accomplished young lady, and ----

Lady. Hear me out son.- Miss Silvester is not less celebrated for her beauty, than for her wit; and, what is above every other consideration, she possesses all the excellencies of the heart. Her fortune I say nothing of, capital as it is; though that would be an object of prime consideration with many a mother.

Son. The observation is too true, but there are few such mothers as mine. I wish, for the honor of human nature, there were thousands of half her merit.

Lady. I did not ask for a compliment, Son, but I thank you for it. – Miss Silvester is---

Son. Let me spare you, Madam, all that you have to say-Miss Silvester is one of the most amiable of her sex- You wish me to visit her- I obey- but there is no merit in this obedience; for I have long loved her with the utmost warmth of affection; and have only to beg your pardon for concealing this circumstance from your knowledge.

Lady. It is easy to pardon, when the offence, if it may be called such, meets with our fullest approbation; but I could wish you had sooner mentioned this circumstance, as it would have added to the happiness of my life.

Son. Diffidence, and fear of offending, alone prevented my doing it; but I hope the present knowledge of our affection (for it is mutual) will contribute to the lengthening that valuable life.

Lady. All obliging as you ever were, Frederic, this compliment comes with peculiar grace. I should suppose a young lady, flattered by her lover, could not be better pleased than a mother thus politely treated by her son. You will visit Miss Silvester, and ---

Son. Our hearts, madam, perfectly accord. – We wanted but an opportunity of making you the confident of our love. Happy Son! Happy Daughter! I hope I shall soon say, in having such a confident.

Lady. Let me add to your happiness, by adding, that Sir Timothy is as eager for his dear daughter's marriage, as I am for yours; and that we have concerted how we should bring about the match with the least violence to your inclinations; and with the strictest regard to the delicacy of the young lady; but since you are already on terms of such intimacy, less ceremony will be necessary.

Son. Expedite, I beseech you, Madam, the happy day; and thereby add to all the obligations you have laid on your Son.

Conversation the Second.
Between a Young Lady and her Lover.

Lover. I have long wished for the opportunity of engaging you in conversation; and since, Madam, -

Lady. Bless me, Sir! I cannot conceive your meaning. Your intimacy in this family gives you continual opportunities of conversing –

Lover. That I acknowledge, Madam; but the presence of a third person has hitherto confined me to general subjects, when my sentiments claimed the attention of yourself in particular.

Lady. You must excuse me, then, if I retire; for it will not be prudent in me to listen to what you think improper to be heard by a third person.

Lover. For heaven's sake favor me with your attention for a few minutes; and be assured, Madam, that I mean not to violate the respect that is due to your character. All my hopes of future happiness depend on your determination – to encourage or discountenance my pretensions. I will not offend your delicacy, by urging this matter farther at present- all I now have to request is, that you will give me room to hope –

Lady. Your behaviour, Sir, is so extremely mysterious –

Lover-.Oh my dear Maria, you must forgive me if I say, you are now guilty of a little dissimulation. Have not my eyes expressed the language of my heart? How often, when

I have half suppressed a rising sigh, has my Maria kindly endeavoured to relieve my agony, by some more than usually familiar expression. She is more endeared to me by such tenderness; for, even admitting the cause to be unknown, the benevolent wish to afford a moment's alleviation to distress, cannot fail to excite gratitude and esteem.

Lady. I pretend no claim upon your gratitude, Sir; but I shall always think myself happy in your esteem. However, I am still ignorant of the purpose you have in view.

Lover. My view, then, is to make amends for the misery I have so long suffered, by securing to myself the greatest happiness this life can afford. To be plain, Madam, I have long entertained a passion for you, that is incapable of increase or decay, and if I shall prove to be so fortunate as to obtain your hand in marriage, it will become my duty, as it is already my inclination, to reward your generous condescension by an unremitting endeavour, to obviate every circumstance that shall threaten to interrupt the harmony of the marriage state.

Lady. Sir, I will candidly acknowledge that I have no partiality towards another; but you are not thence to infer that I make a declaration in favor of yourself.

Lover. Thus, on my knees, permit me to thank you for this inestimable favor.

Lady. Do not deceive yourself, Sir, remember, I said I had not declared in your favor. There are those to whom I am bound in the strongest ties of gratitude and duty; and be assured, that I will never encourage the addresses of a man who has not the sanction of their full approbation.

Lover. I will tomorrow wait upon, and fully explain myself to your father who, I am happy to say, honors me so far as to rank me among the number of his particular friends. In the mean time, Madam, I must beg you to believe that it will be impossible for me to discharge any of the duties of life with so much satisfaction, as those which will contribute to render your happiness complete. And now, Madam, I must humbly take my leave.

Conversation the Third
Between a Father and his Daughter.

Fath. The infirmities of age, my dear Harriet, heavily oppress me; and though to part with a daughter so tenderly and so deservedly beloved, would be a circumstance infinitely more afflicting than to part with life, were it not for the consideration that her happiness-

Daugh. Pardon me, dear Sir, for the interruption; and let me beg you will no longer indulge these melancholy ideas-

Fath. You are mistaken, my Dear, if you suppose that I indulge melancholy, because I express a serious concern for promoting your welfare; therefore be not distressed; but rest assured, that I cherish the hope of living to enjoy greater happiness than I have known for many years.

Daugh. Oh! Sir, you now relieve me from a great anxiety, for the solemnity of your manner gave me terrible apprehensions that something had happened to afflict you.

Fath. No, Harriet, the common accidents of life cannot disturb my repose, while I am possessed of your tender regard, which has been, and I hope will continue to be, the support of my declining years. But I have now a matter to communicate that will claim your particular attention. Mr. Williamson has assured me that he entertains a great affection for you, and has made offers of marriage.

I declined a definitive answer, which I can only give when you have told me whether you approve, or are averse to the alliance; for, as I have often intimated, though perhaps not in express terms, I mean not to put any restraint upon your inclination in a matter of this nature, where a mutual approbation will prove the strongest bond for insuring a lasting felicity.

Daugh. This generosity is too much. It is my duty to submit to your superior judgment. Let me but know your pleasure, and I will, in every instance, implicitly obey, however great the sacrifice.

Fath. I thank you, my Dear, for this proof of your duty. But do not suppose that I wish for an implicit obedience, unless such obedience perfectly accords with the sentiments of your heart. But I will more fully explain myself. I have observed that your behaviour to Mr. Morton has been perfectly easy and familiar, and that you have treated Mr. Williamson with formality and reserve. Now, though I have no material objection to urge against Mr. Morton, I must confess that I should rather approve of the other for a son-in-law. But in this case you are to decide; and I particularly request that you will consult your own, rather than my inclination; for were I to influence you to a choice that you should afterwards regret, the remnant of my life would be passed in an uninterrupted scene of remorse and misery.

Daugh. Heaven forbid that I should so far degenerate from those principles in which I have been educated, as to prefer my own happiness to that of so tenderly indulgent a parent. Dear Sir, recall the power you have transferred to me of that parental authority, which it will ever be my greatest pleasure to obey.

Fath. Nay, my Dear, let us understand each other more clearly. Have you not a partiality for Mr. Morton?

Daugh. I have not, Sir: believe me, marriage has not yet employed my thoughts. I wish but still to live with my kind pappa; to have no care, but, by an innocent trifling, to add some pleasure in his hours of amusement, and to administer comfort in those of distress.

Fath. But I anxiously wish to see you established in life; and when that takes place, I shall think all my cares are at an end. If you are inclined to favor Mr. Morton rather than Mr. Williamson, let not what I have intimated in behalf of the latter, prove an obstacle to the continuance of his addresses.

Daugh. Mr. Morton, Sir, has made no overtures of the nature you allude to; we behave to each other with the familiarity that is usual among persons who have been acquainted from infancy. My reserve to Mr. Williamson, is in consequence of his having made a declaration of love; for I should think myself unworthy to be called your daughter, could I be guilty of such disingenuity of conduct as to afford the least encouragement to a man wanting the essential merit of so revered a parent's recommendation.

Fath. Then, my Dear, he no longer wants that recommendation: – but if you have any other objection –

Daugh. I have none, Sir: but, on the contrary, I will freely confess that I have ever esteemed Mr. Williamson the most accomplished, and, indeed, the most deserving gentleman of my acquaintance.

Fath. A man of mean desert should not rob me of my Harriet. But we must now wave the subject; for our visitors are arrived.

Conversation the Fourth.
Between a Guardian and his Ward.

Guard. I have observed, my dear Emily, that you have been unusually reserved of late; that you are not the sociable companion you used to be; that you avoid all agreeable intercourse; creep into holes and corners; and are, in a word, a very different creature from what you was before we went to Tunbridge. What can be the occasion of all this, my Dear?

Ward. Am I reserved, Sir? —Am I unsociable? – Do I creep into holes and corners? – These are strange charges, Sir. I hope I have done nothing to incur your displeasure.

Guard. Displeasure! my dear. Nothing that my Emily does can ever displease me. She is incapable of real or intentional offence. – But I thought that something sat heavy at your heart, and was anxious to have relieved it; for a more liberal heart never expanded the human bosom.

Ward. Ah, Sir! You are too good. But I fear there is perverseness in that heart that will have but an ill claim to your generosity.

Guard. What mean you, my Love? Only speak your sentiments with freedom, and you shall find how ready I will be to gratify every reasonable wish of your heart:-You shall find in me a second father.

Ward. I have always found one, Sir.- Though I have long lost my own father, I have never known the want of that endearing relation; and, from my earliest remembrance, have had a father in every thing but the name.

Guard. Your father and I were friends, Emily; which would be a sufficient reason for my kindest protection of the daughter, her own merits out of the question. But to the purpose;

I am sure that you are uneasy, and I more than half suspect the cause. Shall I be more explicit?

Ward. You need not, you need not, good Sir. I am sensible to all your kindness, and think your openness of behaviour a call upon my frankness.- In a word, Sir, I find myself very uneasy of late, without being well able to account for the cause of that uneasiness.

Guard. Love, my Dear---

Ward. I know not what the passion means; or, if I now feel it, I have been hitherto a stranger to its impulses.

Guard. You saw Sir Thomas Savile at Tunbridge, my Emily.

Ward. I did, Sir, but---

Guard. No qualifying, Emily – You regarded him with particular marks of attention, and more eyes than mine were upon you; in short, your best friends are of opinion, that you have a strong prepossession in favor of Sir Thomas.

Ward. I confess that he is a very agreeable gentleman---

Guard. And he thinks you a very agreeable girl, Emily---

Ward. Sir!

Guard. In a word, my Dear—I saw your attachment- I have conversed with Sir Thomas- he is greatly enamoured of you; and, if you have no objection, he will visit us on the most friendly terms to-morrow.

Ward. This, Sir, is compelling a confession –You are my guardian, my friend, and my father- I submit to your will-

Guard. Say, rather, your own, Emily. In a word, your inclination shall be consulted; and happy I am to say that it corresponds with the wishes of your best friends, among the warmest of whom you may reckon your guardian.

Ward. Your kindness, Sir, has always prevented my wishes, and the present instance of it will engage my lasting gratitude.

CARDS OF COMPLIMENT,
Proper to be used by Lovers.

I

Mr. Sharp's compliments to Miss Jansen, and he informs her, that he shall consider himself infinitely obliged, if she will alter her resolution of not going to the theatre this evening. He has fortunately learnt that her aunt means to retire immediately after the play; therefore, during the pantomime, Mr.Sharp will have an opportunity of pursuing the theme he entered upon last night, which he is exceedingly anxious to do, as all his hopes of happiness depend on the success of his overtures to the most amiable of her sex.

II

Miss Jansen has heard that love and reason are strangers; and she thinks Mr. Sharp may be classed among the devotees of the former, since he could think Miss Jansen capable of such gross impropriety of conduct, as to remain at the theatre after her aunt had retired, especially as the old lady is in so precarious a state of health. Mr.Sharp will not be an unwelcome guest at the tea-table to-morrow afternoon.

III

The gentleman who will have the honour of delivering this, will answer such questions as Miss Story may think proper to propose respecting Mr. Atkinson, who, assured that neither his moral character or temper can reasonably be objected to, solicits the honor of being permitted to wait upon Miss Story, in order to assure her of the fervency of his esteem.

IV

Sir Henry Lucas, who delivered Mr.Atkinson's card, spoke in very high, and, doubtless, in an equally just, strain of recommendation concerning Mr. Atkinson, whom Miss Story respects as a gentleman of uncommon merit; and she has, therefore, the less scruple of candidly declaring that she is already engaged to a gentleman whom she has every reason to believe worthy her most particular esteem.

V

The indissoluble bond is to be tied tomorrow, between Miss Smithson and Mr.Harley, who unite to request the honor of Mrs. Blewitt's company at breakfast in Hanover-square, thence to proceed to St.George's church.

VI

Mrs. Blewitt will do herself the honor of attending Miss Smithson and Mr.Harley at breakfast to-morrow; and will consent to go to St.George's church, provided Miss Smithson and Mr.Harley will attend there while the indissoluble knot is tied between Mrs.Blewitt and Mr.Simpson, who have agreed to alter their day, that the same hour may give happiness to four of the best of friends.

VII

The compassionate terms in which Miss Knowles spoke of the distressed family, has greatly endeared her to Mr.Moore, who cannot see her without discovering something new in her character to approve and admire. He begs the inclosed trifles may be conveyed to the objects of her generous concern, and to say that he never parts with money with so little regret as when to alleviate affliction.

VIII

Mr.Moore's handsome present was received by the unfortunate people with the utmost gratitude. It was more than sufficient for present exigencies; and to the overplus Miss Knowles has made a small addition for the purpose of re-establishing them in their business.

IX

Mr.Short begs to dance with Miss Fretful tomorrow evening.

X

Miss Fretful received Mr.Short's laconic epistle: but as he has of late so much pleaded the want of time, cannot but wonder that he can make it convenient to be at the masquerade. She must be excused dancing, but Mr. Short will not be displeased to have the opportunity of a more agreeable partner.

XI

Mr.Fairfield's most respectful compliments wait upon Mrs,Saunders; and he entreats that she will permit him to attend her this evening, that he may speak more explicitly on the subject of the alliance he had the honor to propose on Wednesday evening.

XII

When Mr.Fairfield made the proposal alluded to, Mrs.Saunders imagined that he only meant to indulge his usual jocularity; but finding him to have been serious, she assures him that she must entirely decline Mr. Fairfield's overtures.

XIII

The behaviour of Mr.Stamford, at the Opera last night, was too palpably insulting to pass unobserved by Miss Wright, who desires he will not repeat his visits in Stanhope-Street.

XIV

It was extremely painful to engage in conversation with another lady, when Miss Wright was present; but Mr.Stamford had recourse to that expedient, in obedience to Miss Wright's command; for he observed her uncle Morose sitting in the opposite box. This explanation he trusts will remove the prohibition in Miss Wright's card.

XV

Mr. Shatford begs to assure Miss Chadwick, that since he had the honor of attending her home on Tuesday evening, he has waited with the most anxious impatience for the promised appointment; and to request the favor of a line intimating when he may be favored with an interview.

XVI

To get rid of a very troublesome companion, Miss Chadwick was compelled, much against her inclination, to make a promise which she did not mean to fulfil. But, that she may have no further vexation from the same quarter, she declares that in this card she strictly adheres to the truth.

XVII

Mr.Hallifax entreats the favor of Miss Steward's company to-morrow at a dancing-meeting in the Borough. He will wait upon her about seven o'clock,

XVIII

Mr. Hallifax is too much addicted to those vulgar assemblies at public-houses, under the name of dancing-meetings. To frequent them is disgraceful to a man: but renders the character of a woman infamous. If Mr.Hallifax is not engaged in business to-morrow evening, his company will be expected in Friday-Street.

XIX

Miss Whitaker is invited to accompany some of her friends to the Camp on Warley-Common; but she does not mean to go unless Mr.Hume will be of the party.

XX

Mr.Hume is exceedingly obliged to Miss Whitaker for her invitation, which he gratefully accepts: but he expects little happiness from viewing the camp, comparatively with what will arise from spending the day with Miss Whitaker.

XXI

The appointment for Vauxhall must be broke, so unfavourable is the change of weather. Mr. Hall, however, cannot dispense with Miss Wey's company, and will take the liberty of waiting upon her at six this evening.

XXII

Miss Wey will be glad to see Mr. Hall at any time after half past six this evening, being engaged at a neighbour's till that time.

XXIII

Mr. Hampston presents his compliments to Miss Snowden, and hopes for the honor of attending her to Kensington-Gardens on Saturday afternoon.

XXIV

Miss Snowden received Mr. Hampston's card, and expects his company between five and six on Saturday afternoon.

FORMS OF ADDRESS
FOR
PERSONS IN LOVE

To this Division of our little Volume, it may be proper to premise, that nothing is so diffident as genuine Love. We therefore give the following detached sentences, that memory may supply proper phrases in cases where unassisted courage might be wanting.

———

Miss Jackson cannot but know that I have long had a partiality in her favor. If I have never yet expressed my sentiments, she must attribute it to the warmth of those feelings which it is not in language to describe.

"In vain have I struggled. It will not do. My feelings will not be repressed. You must allow me to tell you how ardently I admire and love you." Elizabeth's astonishment was beyond expression. She stared, coloured, doubted, and was silent. This he considered sufficient encouragement, and the avowal of all that he felt and had long felt for her immediately followed.

I should have long before now, Madam, declared my passion, if I had been able to express the generous feelings of an honest heart.

Dear Clarinda, allow me to hope that the ardor with which I have long addressed you, and the repeated proofs I have given of the fervency of my passion, may plead in my behalf, and that I may at length presume so far on your goodness, as to expect the reward of all my sufferings. When will you name the happy day? When shall I prepare the licence and the ring?

I should never suppose that a Girl of my Betsey's delicacy could listen for a moment to the addresses of that odious G_____I am sure she never could entertain a thought so low: and I will therefore flatter myself that I stand well in her opinion.

Animated by the sincerest passion that ever warmed the human breast, permit me to make a full declaration of my Love, in terms as ardent as that Love is sincere: and let me not pray in vain, while I most earnestly solicit a return of your affection: of which I beg you will give me some convincing proof.

If I have offended, I most sincerely ask your pardon: but it was impossible to behold those pouting lips, and not wish to press them:- but if I have offended, I will not offend for nothing-this second kiss shall at once confirm my love, and seal my pardon.

Trust me, Harriot, I am in earnest- I must have an explicit answer- My passion is so fervent that it will no longer bear the pretty triflings of your sex. My sufferings have been extreme-Let your generosity put a period to them.

What can I say, Madam? The more proofs I give of my Love, the more you seem to despise me. Is there never to be a period to my woes?

143

No man ever loved woman as I love you. Reciprocality of affection can alone ensure our mutual happiness. If marriage be your view, as it is mine; say so at once, and let us be happy.

Though your fortune, my Charmer, is superior to mine; yet will I endeavour to repair the deficiency by every tender proof that I can give, that I prefer the happiness of my Charmer to my own.

Life without Love would be a burden: but to love, and not know that we are loved again, produces the most insupportable anxiety. Give me, then, some assurance that I am not wholly indifferent to you, and you will ease my breast of a thousand tortures.

Dearest of Girls, be assured, that large as my fortune is, if it were ten times larger, I would with pride lay it at your feet. Take me, then, for life, and mould me to your wishes. –I shall never be happy till I can call you mine.

Open and frank as your nature is to every one else, why will you act with reserve to me alone?-Is it because I love you beyond all women, that I am to be treated with more severity than any other man?

The diffidence attending genuine Love has hitherto prevented a declaration of my passion, but the long-smothered flame will burst forth; and I must obtain my Amelia's consent to make me happy, or miserable for life.

In a word, my ever charming Letitia, I love you beyond all expression; but I would not make this free declaration of my passion, till I had obtained your father's consent: – On your decree, then, depends my future fate.

I have a favor to ask of you, Madam, that demands your private ear. Will you walk with me to the woodbine alcove, and I will explain myself more fully.

Ravished as my heart first was by your beauty, I am now still more charmed with your virtues. Your character rises on me every moment. An union with you, then, my loved Eliza, as it is the first wish of my heart, so it is the only mode by which that heart can be made happy. Accept my vows, and my life shall all be devoted to the promotion of your happiness.

We honest Tars, Nancy, speak our minds. If you will have me, say so. I will range the wide world to bring home treasure for my lovely Girl.

PROPER FORMS OF REPLY
to be used by the
FEMALE SEX.

You talk like a man of honor and a gentleman; and therefore you have my consent to speak on this subject to me father.

There is so much of extravagance in your professions, that I really imagine, Sir, you mean to make me an object of ridicule. I insist that you affront me no more, and assure you that I will never consent to admit your address.

I have no doubt, Sir, of your expectations in life being very favorable; but wealth cannot give happiness to those whose minds do not accord. Our tempers are so opposite that we could scarcely avoid disagreements on the most trifling occasions: to be connected in marriage, therefore, would give no prospect of content to either, but be productive of eternal remorse.

You say you will explain yourself. I wish for no explanation on the subject you have introduced. I shall continue to esteem you as a common acquaintance, but desire you will avoid attempting to engage me hereafter in a particular conversation; for I am determined to give no countenance to your addresses.

I am entirely at a loss, Sir, in what manner to reply. Could I be assured of your sincerity, I would not hesitate – but time must prove whether you deserve to be considered as such an adherent to truth as you represent yourself to be.

I cannot promise what you desire, without being guilty of manifest ingratitude and indiscretion. It is both my inclination and duty to consult my friends on all matters of consequence. However, I will acknowledge, that your greatest difficulty will be in obtaining their concurrence: for you will not be very obstinately opposed by me.

Your politeness, Sir, is more conspicuous than your sincerity; and I cannot imagine that I possess any of those charms which you are pleased to attribute to me.

I have learnt from unquestionable authority, that you are already under engagements to Miss Johnson; and am amazed at your effrontery in addressing me on this subject. I am determined to see you no more; and if we may hereafter meet by accident, an unwillingness to attract observation only, will prevent my immediately withdrawing.

Be assured, Sir, that I will never engage in a clandestine correspondence: and your endeavouring to persuade me into so imprudent a measure, has given me no favourable opinion of your intentions.

I cannot fix the day; for I fear the day you refer to will never arrive. Notwithstanding the fervency of your declaration, I have but too much reason to doubt your fidelity.

Indeed, my dear Harry, I am concerned that you should suppose the unhappy change of your fortune would alter my affection. No; I am convinced of your integrity; and to-morrow shall give you possession of your Harriot, and a greater fortune than you ever expected she would have the happiness of bestowing upon him she thinks the most deserving of his sex.

I cannot comply with your request; but hope you will not think I mean to affront you, Sir, when I declare, that I am prepossessed in favour of another.

Your behaviour, Sir, is extremely candid. As to your question respecting the licence and the ring, I confess they are necessary preliminaries; but you know, if they are procured to night, it does not follow, that I must be precipitated into the confines of marriage to-morrow.

As to the particular church, Sir, I am indifferent: though I must confess, that I wish not the ceremony to be made public: therefore, I would rather have the knot tied at some distance from town, in one of the places where your residence has been long enough to give you the title of an inhabitant.

I have unfortunately countenanced your pretensions, which I now sincerely regret, and must insist that you decline your visits; for your general character is too bad to admit of excuse or palliation, and I fear you act from a confirmed habit of vice, rather than fall into casual indiscretions.

Your conduct since I have had the happiness of your acquaintance, has been unexceptionable in every respect, and if I decline a positive declaration of love, be assured that you are not indifferent to me.

I am sorry, Sir, to say any thing that I suppose will give you uneasiness; but my father has, for reasons known, he says, only to himself, forbid the continuance of your visits.

I consent, Sir, to obtain your addresses, on the condition that you obtain my Aunt's concurrence.

LOVE LETTERS IN VERSE
To Maria

To thee, my fair, these lines I dare impart,
The faithful picture of a feeling heart.
When first thy beauties caught my ravish'd view,
I gaz'd, I wonder'd, and I lov'd thee too.
From that dear moment all my peace was lost,
And love and solitude my only boast
Sleep fled my eyes, nor books, nor friends could charm,
And my fond heart for thee alone was warm:
Each beating pulse, and every rising sigh,
But serv'd to tell Maria was not nigh:
My shivering limbs and half dissolving frame,
Proclaim'd the power of her all-charming name.
Her charming name now vibrates in my ears:
But ah! the lovely maid no more appears.

Born to the Bath, where belles and beaux appear,
How little knows she of her Henry's care!
How little feels the fierce corroding pains,
That rend his breast, and vibrate thro' his veins!
Alas! she feels not how his mind is tost,
And every hope, with dear Maria, lost!
Yet, if these lines her tender breast invade,
And, for one moment, warm the lovely maid,
Henry will hope to see the happy day,
When, blithe as morn, and fragrant as the May,
He to the temple shall Maria lead,
And in the wife shall lose the darling maid:

Then happy will his future days be spent,
And all his life be love, and sweet content.

Henry.

The Lady's Answer
Fond swain, thy letter is receiv'd,
And all its warm contents believ'd:
Maria knows, and feels by turns,
What flame in Henry's bosom burns.
For Ah! She owns an equal flame,
Which till this hour she dar'd not name.

The Bath for me no charm will prove,
While absent from the man I love,
Nor belles nor beaux that flutter here,
Need give thy breast a moment's care;
That faithful breast I know is mine,
And to its ardors I resign.

Soon shall the flying steeds convey
From fools and cripples, sick and gay,
From fancied pains, and real woes.
And all the ills that Fortune knows,
Thy lov'd Maria to thy arms;
And then, if she has any charms,
Those charms may Henry boast his own,
Possess unrivall'd and alone.

Maria.

To Lavinia
My Dear Lavinia let us stray,
And revel in the sweets of May;

Not May herself in beauty bright,
Can give the shepherd more delight,
As through the fragrant field he roves,
Revolving o'er his happy loves,
Than the dear mention of thy name,
To him who owns an equal flame.

What, though our fortunes differ wide?
My wealth, and all I boast beside,
Are wholly thine: an honest heart,
A temper liberal to impart:
A soul that feels for every woe;
And feeling, would relieve it too.
Ample my store in wealth and land;
The master —all — at thy command;
A dearer treasure thou, than e'er
Has yet engag'd thy Damon's care.

Then come, dear Maid, in all thy charms,
And yield thee to thy Lover's arms;
The church our holy vows shall seal;
My future life shall seek thy weal;
Each passing day shall amply prove
The warmth and ardor of my love.

Come then, Lavinia, let us stray,
And revel in the sweets of May.

Damon.

The Reply.
What, my Damon, can I say?
How enjoy the sweets of May?

How shall I, a maiden poor,
Dare infringe on Damon's store?
If, indeed, by fortune blest,
I could give him ease or rest;
Could his gen'rous pains relieve;
Nothing that I had to give,
Should I think a price too high,
Damon's honest heart to buy.

But, as fortune has denied
Riches worthy of thy bride;
Let me now thy vows reject,
Professing love and warm respect;
Wishing still increase of wealth,
Increase of honour and of health;
And every joy that life can give;
Though poor Lavinia still must live
Solemn and sad to make her moan,
And sigh unfriended and alone.

Lavinia.

To Lavinia,

No, my Lavinia, lovely maid
Ah no! it never shall be said,
That paltry fortune could destroy
The promis'd harvest of our joy.

Whate'er I have, – myself, is thine,
To thee this moment I resign.
The licence and the ring are bought;
The rest is rapture but in thought.

Come then, Lavinia, to my arms,
And (flush'd in all thy native charms)
Let sordid souls a match behold,
Uninfluenc'd by the weight of gold.

Thus, bound by every grateful tie,
With thee I'll live, with thee I'll die:
Nor shalt thou e'er have cause to moan,
Or sigh unfriended and alone.

Damon.

The Final Answer
What, my Damon, can I say?
(The licence bought, and fix'd the day)
To thee and Love I must resign;
And may the hour that makes thee mine,
Unusually propitious prove,
To such a tried and honest Love.
For me, I always will, as now,
Obedience, grateful duty, vow:
And if the warmest wish to please;
Thy happiness to seek, thy ease;
In sickness and in health to tend,
A wife, a lover, and a friend;
If these my duties may repay
The obligations of this day,
Then shall I think me wholly blest,
And leave to Heaven and thee the rest:
For all my future life shall prove
My sense of gratitude and love.

Lavinia.

From a Gentleman to a Lady, on Valentine's Day.

Let my gentle Valentine
Now declare she will be mine;
Many a month and many a day,
Have I pin'd my soul away;
Hoping each propitious hour,
As it shew'd my Jesse's power,
Would my Jesse's love declare,
And bless me with the charming fair:
But if Jesse's heart be froze,
Strephon is not one of those,
Who, to carking care a prey,
Will consume the tedious day;
Or through midnight hours proclaim
His love for one unworthy dame.
No – if the girl I fondly love,
Takes causeless pains her hate to prove;
Then will I seek another maid,
Of truth and honour not afraid.
I will be her's while she is mine,
To her my heart I will resign,
And she shall be my Valentine.

The Lady's Answer.

No – Jesse is not one of those,
Whose hard unfeeling hearts are froze;
Who treats a lover with disdain,
And feels a joy in giving pain;
Nor is she blind to Strephon's merits,
But owns the virtues he inherits;
Nor has she strove her heart to prove,

Tho' she has long conceal'd her love,
To try if he would persevere,
And thereby proves his vows sincere.
And since sincere he seems to be,
Manly and honest, frank and free,
He need not seek another Fair,
Nor waste his days in pining care;
But if he feels his heart inclin'd
To seek his Jesse, he may find
This day, to prove her not unkind.

ACROSTIC.

L – ove, of all the generous passions,
O – nly warms the gentle breast;
V – ast and fond its inclinations
E – ver warring – ne'er at rest.

ANOTHER.

J – oin'd for life, why should I vex?
E – ver charming is the sex.
A – ll the powers of Love are theirs,
L – ove and all its tender cares.
O – ft of slighted love I deem;
U – seless find I all my dream:
S – urely all my doubts are vain;
Y – e winds, I yield them back again!

ANOTHER.

C – ould you, cruel maiden, say
O – ught that should my breast alarm,
U – nless, you mean to give away
R – espect as gen'rous as 'tis warm?
T – ry me by each holy test;
S – acred vows shall seal the rest.

H – appy could I hail the hour,
I – n which Hymen shews his power,
P – roud on your head each bliss to shower.

ANOTHER.

M – an was made to serve the sex;
A – ll the cares this life perplex,,
R – ightly on his shoulders fall,
R-ightly he sustains them all.
I – n the course of love we find,
A – ll-engaging woman kind,
G – iven by Heav'n to smooth his care,
E – ver charming, kind, and fair.

REBUS.

The letter for fifty, and that like the globe,
With another for five often found,
And the first of the name of Old England's brave queen,
Who thunder'd her cannons around;
These letters, in happy conjunction, will shew
The sweetest of passions that mortals can know.

ANOTHER.

The place where kings and queens abide,
And what rolls nobly o'er the tide:-
These words in combination will display
The pretty trifling of the youthful day.

ANOTHER.

A thing that is us'd when laid down at a door,
And two-fifths of what every one praises,
With the thing all will strive for, who would not be poor,
Which the heart of its owner still raises.
Add these together, and you'll see
A happy state of life,

If those who know it, can agree
To keep out noise and strife.

CONCLUSION.

And thus our little volume's ended,
In which such various things are blended,
As, studied well, will teach the Lover,
He never ought to be a rover.

The maid may learn in many a part,
To save her pride and guard her heart.
For through the work our wishes warm,
Have been to guard the sex from harm:
Dear sex! – the solace of our lives,
As mothers, daughters, maids or wives.

How comfortless the man would roam
Without the solace of a home,
Where female sweetness still appears,
To bless him with her softest cares;
To smile away all cause of strife,
And smooth the rugged road of life.

The youth enamoured may be taught
How cheaply real bliss is bought;
That honor points the road to wealth,
And honest Love to lasting health.

Let men and maids, then, all agree,
That MARRIAGE IS TRUE LIBERTY:
With cautious heed, O let them shun
The ways which thousands have undone:

And learn, that as they hope the joys,
Of beauteous girls, and prattling boys,
That all of truly good and great
Is center'd in the MARRIED STATE.

Let those who read our honest page,
Commend it to the RISING AGE;
So shall our labors gain their end,
At once to pleasure and amend.
FINIS.

Action for a Breach of Promise of Matrimony.
(*The New Lady's Magazine or Companion for the Fair Sex*, February 1787)

On Saturday came on in the Court of Common Pleas, a trial wherein Charles Bourne, Gentleman, was plaintiff, and the Countess de Crequi Lanaples was defendant.

This was an action upon a breach of promise of marriage, and the plaintiff laid his damages at 20,000l.

It appeared by the evidence that the plaintiff was, at the commencement of his courtship, a young man and lieutenant of marines, with only his pay, and a pension of fifty pounds per annum, to support him.

That the defendant, whose name is Comerford, was a native of Ireland, and relict to a foreign Count, at whose death she came into possession of a considerable personal fortune, and had seventeen thousand pounds in the British funds.

That the plaintiff had been acquainted with her for a considerable time; had introduced her to several friends as a lady he was about to marry. That he informed a friend in her presence, that she had promised to settle ten thousand

In the gallery there were many family portraits, but they could
have little to fix the attention of a stranger. Elizabeth walked on in
quest of the only face whose features would be known to her. At
last it arrested her – and she beheld a striking resemblance of Mr
Darcy, with such a smile over the face as she remembered to have
sometimes seen when he looked at her. She stood several minutes
before the picture, in earnest contemplation, and returned to it again
before they quitted the gallery. Mrs Reynolds informed them that it
had been taken in his father's lifetime.

pounds upon him, and procure him a seat in Parliament, and that returning from Shepperton in a coach with some other friends, he told them, the Countess had promised to make him happy on the 15th September, upon which she observed, "that is a remarkable day to me, for on that day I was married to the Count."

That on making this observation, a young lady present offered to be her bridesmaid, for which she thanked her; then another lady present made up clothes for the occasion, and the defendant said she had white clothes which would answer.

But it also appeared that through all these conversations the Countess never gave an express promise, though she never contradicted what Mr. Bourne asserted in her presence to be her sentiments.

It also appeared, that on complaint being made of Mr. Bourne's neglecting his duty, the defendant declared her intention to place him on a more elevated situation, wished he should never more join his corps, and that he soon after gave up his rank, and retired upon half pay.

Lord Loughborough, in his charge to the jury, observed, that there were two questions for their consideration, 1stly – Whether the evidence amounted to a cause of action; 2dly – if they thought it did, what damages the plaintiff was entitled to.

The Jury brought in a verdict for the plaintiff, with one shilling damages.

A MATRIMONIAL ANECDOTE.
(The New Lady's Magazine or Companion for the Fair Sex, May 1787)

In an age when matrimony is too often made a mere matter of money, the following, which from good authority is given us as a fact, stands a striking exception: A noble Duke, the first in point of youth and fortune in the kingdom, being lately down at an assembly in Gloucestershire, saw a lady of such beauty and accomplishments, that he immediately fell in love with her, and as soon made proposals of marriage to her father. The old gentleman felt the pride of such an alliance too deeply to refuse his consent, and introduced him to his daughter, who with great politeness thanked his Grace for his intentions, but said, that as her happiness was built upon other foundations than the glare of rank, she must decline the honour of his hand.

This refusal creating a very great surprise both in the father and lover, an investigation took place, when it appeared the young lady's affections were engaged to a neighbouring gentleman of about 1000l. per year; the Duke gave up his pretensions, and the father, like a man of sense, had added to the triumph of affection over title, by giving his consent to the intended union.

The father of the young lady is no more than what is called a gentleman farmer, but worth above 100,000l., and she is his only child.

Poems from *The Lady's Magazine* (1786 and 1797)
The Despairing Lover

I

Most rigid fate! Is this my destin'd lot;
For ever thus to be by you forgot.
O! cruel maid, in pity lend an ear,
And drop with me one sympathizing tear;
Assuage my grief, drive anguish from my mind,
And let me in you some compassion find.

II

But why do I thus of my fate complain,
She hears me not with pleasure, but disain,
Soft pity from her breast is far remov'd.
My fate's to love, but not to be belov'd.
Can death alone then ease me of my grief!
Then death shall speedily give me relief.

III

No longer here do I desire to live,
The world to me no lasting joys can give;
A thousand times I'd rather choose to die
Than live in dire despair and misery.
The tortures of my soul no hope can tell
No pity ease, no lively mirth dispel.

E____ N____

Lines Addressed to a Lady by her Admirer

Dear Madam, you know,
Some few days ago.
Unto you a billet was sent;
With impatience I burn'd
But no answer return'd
Which causes me much to relent.

For had I been told,
Don't think me too bold,
That you ever so fickle would prove,
I as soon would believe
Birds their young ones would leave
Or the eagle would nest with the dove.

But my sweet pretty miss,
The reason seems this,
Your admirers increasing in number,
Poor S is thrown by,
Like a pig in a stye,
And am thought of no more than old lumber.
WILMOT

Directions for the Choice of a Loving Husband
(*The Lady's Magazine*, August 1786)

"Silence is eloquence in love" – This is my text and I shall endeavour to make as few digressions as possible; but should an unconnected observation drop from my pen (as is often the case with modern writers), I flatter myself it will be overlooked. I shall now proceed to convince my fair readers, that the man who is embarrassed and nearly deprived of utterance, when in the presence of the woman who has sole possession of his thoughts, is truly in love: ergo, the coxcomb who is never abashed in the presence of her who believes his pretended regard to be sincere, and is ever supplied with an inexhaustible fund of nonsense (amongst the fashionable called small-talk), which he well knows will be agreeable to the object of his momentary attention- his love is clearly the reverse. We too often find the man who follows this base and unmanly pursuit, entangle the heart of her he never wooed with honourable intentions: whilst the man of the first description, whose intention is nothing but marriage (such as religion and conjugal felicity point out) rejected by the woman, who had made the external appearance only of the two her peculiar attention; little suspecting that the silent man could deserve her esteem, and that the deceitful villain, whom she would most willingly give her hand to, ought to be avoided as a monster, that is lurking till its prey can be seized to advantage-

Those females who have been deceived by such flatterers, may perhaps, as an apology for their imprudence, allege that he was formed to win their hearts; but here let me observe to them, that the other person, allowing him not to be so handsome as they might wish (if not so ugly that his horse would start at his approach), deserves their preference much: and it is very little in favour of their sex, to say their hearts are to be won by a fine shape, face or suit of cloaths. I will be more lenitive, and impute it to his power of speech, and skill in the art of making love, which enabled him to make such false protestations, as induced the unguarded to believe his professions sincere. I shall here introduce a narrative which I can give as fact, being well acquainted with the parties. Maria, a young lady of beauty, about eighteen, of gay notions, the daughter of a cheesemonger, who, I suppose could give her a few thousands, had two suitors of very different descriptions. The first who paid his addresses to her was a young fellow, aged about two and twenty, of exceeding good fortune, and a most placid agreeable companion, but had little or nothing to say in her presence, though never at a loss in the company of other women: his love was not divided; however, him she rejected; for what reason? Because she thought he was neither fashionable nor agreeable; he was not fashionable, because he had an aversion to foppery; and not agreeable, as he could never keep up a conversation of any duration of nonsense with her: to his person no objection could she make. – At the disappointment, so great was his chagrin, that he was determined to try that infallible cure, absence and variety: he accordingly made a tour through France, from whence he returned with his heart as sound as ever; made an offer of it and his hand to a very amiable young lady, which she did not think proper to refuse. They have now two children, and I think no pair in England can be happier. The other suitor was an old debaucher, and not a very young man, between thirty and forty, who was ever ready to take advantage of the unsuspecting fair; dressed much, talked more, appeared as a butterfly to men, but an Adonis to women; to give the devil his due, he was very handsome (which he well knew), and was possessed of an independent fortune, that entitled him to a rank amongst the fashionable of this metropolis. In the company of men of letters, not a word could he speak, but in the company of women was ever prating. Such was the man Maria loved, and this was the man she thought agreeable, and a proper companion for life; but she was soon convinced of her error. She was walking with a party rather late one evening, when he found means to lead her astray, and was actually going to force her to comply with his brutal desires, had not her shrieks brought some of the party to her rescue. He expected, without doubt, an easy compliance. Maria has since been obliged to marry a man that I am sure she could never be in love with.

I shall conclude with observing to females in general, that what I have said has only been for their better government.

T.C.G.S.

Advice to the Ladies
(*The Lady's Magazine*, August 1797)

Detest, disguise; remember 'tis your part,
By gentle fondness, to retain the heart.
Let duty, prudence, virtue, take the lead
To fix your choice, – but from it ne'er recede.
Abhor coquetry; spurn the shallow fool

Who measures out dull compliments by rule,
And without meaning, like a chattering jay,
Repeats the same dull strain throughout the day.
Are men of sense attracted by your face,
Your well-turn'd figure, or their compound grace?
Be mild and equal, – moderately gay;
Your judgment rather than your wit display.
By aiming at good-breeding, strive to please;
'Tis nothing more than regulated ease.
Does one dear youth, among the sylvan train,
The best affections of your heart obtain?
And is he reckoned worthy of your choice?
Is your opinion with the general voice?
Confess it then, – nor from him seek to hide
What's known to everybody else beside.
Attach him to you; in a generous mind,
A lively gratitude expect to find.
Receive his love; and, by a kind return,
The blaze, affection, will the brighter burn;
Disdain duplicity; from pride be free:
What every woman should, you then will be.

W_L_ _ _ M G_ _F_ _ D

A Letter from a Seduced Female
(*The Lady's Monthly Museum*, 1800)

To Edward Bernard Esq.

The wretched being who writes this will, ere you receive it, be no more! Then, perhaps, you will repent of your cruelty to her who would willingly have died to promote your happiness. Yes, Edward, for you I left my doting parents – I set at nought the world's opinion to possess your love! Think, then, what

Elizabeth's spirits soon rising to playfulness again, she wanted Mr Darcy to account for his ever having fallen in love with her. "How could you begin? said she. "I can comprehend your going on charmingly, when you had once made a beginning; but what could set you off in the first place." "I cannot fix on the hour, or the spot, or the look, or the words, which laid the foundation. It is too long ago. I was in the middle before I knew that I had begun." "My beauty you had early withstood, and as for my manners – my behaviour to you was at least always bordering on the uncivil, and I never spoke to you without rather wishing to give you pain than not. Now, be sincere, did you admire me for my impertinence?"

agony I must feel when I perused your letter! Was it humane to insult the wretched? No, Edward! Though I once yielded to love, and lost a father's good opinion, never will I sacrifice my own, by becoming what you wish. I have still sufficient virtue to shudder at prostitution!

Yesterday, for the first time since I left his protection, I met my father. He was alone, walking in the park. I threw myself at his feet, and besought his forgiveness. His looks cut me to the heart.

"Let me pass!" said he, while his voice shook with passion.

"First say – you forgive the repentant Rosa!" – and I clasped his knees.

"Never!" said he –"Abandoned girl" – and rushed past me.

For some time I lay senseless. When I recovered, the recollection of his former kindness rendered me nearly frantic. – How often has he pressed me in his arms, and vowed that he could deny his darling Rosa nothing! Oh! How could I remember this, and leave him? Surely my heart then must have been as hard as your's!

Had I obtained my father's forgiveness, I would have strove to live, in spite of the world's censure. But without a friend to encourage my return to virtue – without an acquaintance – for what mother would suffer her daughter to associate with me – can life be worth preserving?

Edward, farewell! – My first and only love – may you live, and repent! Oh! think, when on the bed of death every bad action appears with redoubled horror. How will your conscience be smitten for the unfortunate Rosa! – who, through you, received a father's curse! – and, through your desertion, put an end to her existence.

Once more farewell! That Heaven may shower down its blessings upon you, is the last prayer of

Rosa Somerton

PART TWO

MARRIAGE

The Wedding Ceremony and the Honeymoon

Weddings in late Georgian and Regency England were quiet, private affairs attended by close family and a few friends; even society weddings held in fashionable London churches, such as St George's in Hanover Square, were quiet and understated.

The bride and bridesmaids arrived at the church to the sound of wedding bells, in carriages decorated with ribbons known as 'wedding favours'. The bride did not necessarily wear white; the colour of her dress was a matter of personal choice, and a coloured dress did not denote a lack of virginity. Flowing classical-style dresses in lightweight fabrics, such as sarsenet or muslin, were popular. Bridesmaids often wore white dresses. The groom wore his best suit.

Brides and bridesmaids often used their dresses again after the wedding, as ballgowns or evening dresses. In *Mansfield Park,* when Fanny Price is bridesmaid to her cousin Maria she wears a white dress decorated with glossy spots. Fanny wears this dress again at a dinner party and at the ball Sir Thomas Bertram holds for her and her brother.

The wedding service, which was taken from the Book of Common Prayer, included the bride's promise to obey her husband. Matrimonial rings were exchanged. These were plain or decorated gold bands, often inscribed with the couple's initials and the date of the wedding. The round, never-ending form of the ring was a reminder that the couple's love should circulate and flow continually. It was worn on the fourth finger of the left hand because it was believed that a vein of blood passed from that finger into the heart.

The ceremony was followed by a simple wedding breakfast, which included a wedding cake. Afterwards the couple set off on their honeymoon, which took the form of a wedding journey or bridal tour. A number of places, including seaside resorts and spa towns, were visited on the journey. It was also traditional to visit relatives who had not attended the wedding. The bride's sister or a close female friend often accompanied her on her honeymoon to support her as she embarked on her new life. This happens in *Mansfield Park* when Julia Bertram goes to Brighton with Maria and her new husband.

Another tradition was for the bridegroom to buy a new carriage for himself and his new wife. In *Emma* the recently married Eltons parade around in a new carriage, and in *Persuasion* Captain Wentworth buys his bride 'a very pretty landaulette'.

After the event weddings were announced in newspapers and magazines, such as the *Lady's Magazine*. Jane Austen enjoyed reading marriage announcements and often commented on any she found amusing in letters to her sister.

On their return from honeymoon the newlyweds were fêted in the local community where they were to set up home. Their neighbours traditionally visited them and enjoyed a piece of wedding cake; these visits were returned by the couple. In the weeks following her marriage the new wife was given precedence on entering a room and at social functions, including over those who would normally have precedence over her. As a married woman she would henceforth have precedence over single women, a privilege which Lydia Bennet in *Pride and Prejudice* seizes with alacrity.

There are no lengthy descriptions of the heroine's weddings in Jane Austen's novels. The double wedding of Jane and Elizabeth Bennet is summed up with the words 'Happy for all her maternal feelings was the day on which Mrs Bennet got rid of her two most deserving daughters.' The ill-fated wedding of Maria Bertram and Mr Rushworth in *Mansfield Park* is described in more detail:

It was a very proper wedding. The bride was elegantly dressed – the two bridesmaids were duly inferior – her father gave her away – her mother stood with salts in her hand, expecting to be agitated – her aunt tried to cry – and the service was impressively read by Dr Grant. Nothing could be objected to when it came under the discussion of the neighbourhood, except that the carriage which conveyed the bride and bridegroom and Julia from the church door to Sotherton was the same chaise which Mr Rushworth had used for a twelvemonth before. In everything else the etiquette of the day might stand the strictest investigation.

The wedding of Jane Austen's niece Anna and Ben Lefroy, which took place on a cold, grey morning in

November 1814, was typical of weddings at that time. The ceremony in St Nicholas Church, Steventon, was a very quiet event attended by just close family members.

Anna wore a white muslin dress, a fringed silk shawl embossed with white flowers and a cap trimmed with lace. The two small bridesmaids wore white dresses and straw bonnets decorated with white ribbons. There were no flowers to brighten the gloomy church.

A simple wedding breakfast was held after the ceremony. The guests were served bread, hot rolls, buttered toast, cold meat and eggs. There was also a chocolate cake and a wedding cake.

The newlyweds, who did not have a honeymoon, left soon after the wedding breakfast to drive to their new home in Hendon.

Happily Ever After (Hopefully)

The lives of women of the middle and upper classes were focused on their husbands, families and homes. As marriage was effectively their career, it was very important, if not essential, to make it work. Marriage was also for life; in the words of Catherine Morland, the heroine of *Northanger Abbey*, 'People that marry can never part.'

There was little chance of ending an unhappy marriage; women were not allowed to divorce their husbands and men could only divorce their wives in exceptional circumstances. Divorce was extremely expensive and an Act of Parliament was required for each case. It also resulted in scandal, disgrace and ruined reputations. In the rare instances in which it occurred, divorce was especially disastrous for women, who lost everything, including their children.

The divorce of the Rushworths in *Mansfield Park* causes a great scandal and is reported in the London papers, much to the distress of the Bertram family. Due to the double standards of that time, Maria is punished with social ostracism for her part in the collapse of her marriage while Henry Crawford, who is equally responsible, escapes punishment.

Conduct books and advice manuals for women had much to say on the best way to achieve marital happiness. There was plenty of guidance on how women should keep their husbands happy by being good wives, mothers, hostesses, housekeepers and managers of servants. Some emphasized the importance of keeping passion alive. All of the advice literature agreed on the necessity of working hard to achieve a happy marriage.

Achieving this was not easy at a time when many women were forced to marry for economic reasons and to avoid the ignominy of spinsterhood. Not all women were lucky enough to marry a man they loved and respected. Some took the risk of marrying a man to secure a home of their own and financial security, and trusted that love would come afterwards.

Jane Austen's belief that unions based on love, respect and a thorough knowledge of each other were the most likely to lead to marital happiness is illustrated by the stories of her heroines. This belief was, no doubt, influenced by the example of her parents' marriage. George and Cassandra Austen were a well-suited couple and their marriage was a happy and successful one. The sensible, well-educated, clever and witty Cassandra was the perfect wife for the gentle, placid, cheerful, scholarly and amiable George. There were also a number of other happy marriages in Jane's family, including those of four of her brothers and her uncle and aunt, James and Jane Leigh-Perrot, who were a close and devoted couple.

There are several examples of successful marriages in Jane Austen's novels. These include that of the contented and affable Gardiners in *Pride and Prejudice,* and the Crofts in *Persuasion,* who are described as 'particularly attached and happy'. The Westons in *Emma*, although only recently married, seem a particularly well-suited couple whose marriage is described as showing 'every promise of happiness'.

A Mother to her Daughter – Just on the Point
of Marriage
(*The Lady's Monthly Museum*, February 1804)

Your situation, my beloved child, at the moment when I am about to resign you into the arms of another, is calculated to awaken every tender feeling, and to arouse all the delicious, yet anxious energies of material sensation; to recall to fond remembrance, the period, when I thought the throes I had just endured, amply repaid, by receiving you into this bosom. These arms have hitherto fondly cherished you; and, with a solicitude, which you cannot know, till you have passed through the same course of duties, I have watched over you, and directed your every step; I have endeavoured, without intermission, to set you an example; to be as a pattern ever before your eyes, suited to excite in your young heart, an earnest desire of growing up to the same image: in the accomplishment of this, I have constantly aspired after greater degrees of perfection; and whatever may have been my infirmities in the execution of this most important office, I have succeeded in guiding your tender years through the age of inexperience, through the period of new sensations and lively sensibilities, till I am about to place you in the temple of Love and Honor.

It is a great alleviation of the anxiety, which, as your mother, I must experience on the present occasion, that you have enjoyed the full benefit of a virtuous education; of examples of every kind, which can prepare a young woman to be a treasure to her husband; you have a father, whose mild and beneficent exercise of authority must have taught you to wish, that your husband may possess all the prerogatives, which all laws, divine and human, have given him in the headship of his own house, and to remove far from you, every desire of degrading, much more of endeavouring to make him contemptible, by any efforts to usurp his place yourself.

It does not become your mother to say more, than that she has not been a disgrace to her connections.

As you have seen love and harmony reigning between your parents, and shedding their benign influence upon their offspring, so you have participated in the benefits arising therefrom; you have beheld affection and purity, the implantation of nature in the hearts of brothers and sisters towards each other, thus fostered, bring forth goodly fruit: in your brothers, decency in words and actions, gallant behaviour and generous protection towards their sisters ; in your sisters, modesty and every sweet attractive grace. In such society, you have tasted the most cordial endearments that can be derived from the innocent intercommunity of the sexes, serving to confirm, instead of injuring, the deep root which Nature has given to modesty in a female breast.

Thus the fond heart of your mother exults in the prospect of seeing her dear girl exchange her truly virgin charms for the "virgin majesty" of the nuptial state, as your favourite Milton has expressed it; an author, of whom Dr Johnson (no way partial to him) says, that his whole works contain no idea that can pollute the reader's mind: even this, though it may be called negative, is great praise, considering the purposes to which poetry is too often applied.

What woman, in whom innate purity has been preserved, does not feel the inspiring influence of this great poet's applying the term "virgin" to Eve, after her connection with Adam? We here see him joining the youthful bloom, sweetness and innocence of the maid, with the sedateness and divine gravity of the matron; combining sprightliness of the one with the solemnity of marriage vows in the other; the sweet simplicity and chearfulness of the maid with dignity of character and sanctity of condition, in the wife, and making chastity, like the thread of gold in tissue, run through the whole. How has he preserved consistency, whenever he adverts to this subject? Showing that he well understood,

> Whatever hypocrites austerely talk
> Of purity and place and innocence,

that the true idea of chastity can only be formed in the mind in the sacred bond of marriage; that in this great ordinance of nature, the connection between one man and one woman, founded in affection, and inviolably adhered to, purity is carried to its proper pitch, chastity is placed upon its proper basis.

I have chosen to dwell chiefly on that, in which your honor and happiness must principally consist; in which you are made, as it were, the depository of the honor and happiness of your husband, of his family and your own, and of your posterity for generations to come, which would be disgraced by your unworthy conduct, as long as your name was remembered. Do not be alarmed at this weight of honor you are called to sustain; it shall be supported with ease, and the trust discharged with dignity, by my child, taught, as she has been, to respect herself and her father's house, and to reflect upon the claim her sex and society have upon her for her example.

To these powerful motives to duty, will now be superadded, the inexhaustible delight you will find, in constituting the chief earthly felicity, and ministering to the enjoyment, of the worthy man who has preferred you to all your sex; has confided to you the future comfort of his life; has chosen you to be the keeper of his honor, and the mother of his children.

I will not expatiate farther at present, than to express my firm persuasion, that if my life is spared, I shall see my daughter "shine as conspicuously" as a WIFE and MOTHER as she has done in the single state in her father's house.

Marriage Announcements
(*The Lady's Magazine*, August, September and October 1771)

I

By Special Licence at Kensington, Thomas Pitt Esq., Member of Parliament, Oakhampton to Miss Wilkinson of Hanover Square.

Francis Perry Esq. to Miss Fanny Eames niece to John Eames Esq., Member for Newport in the Isle of Wight.

At Deptford, Richard Southby Esq., aged 78 to Miss Sally Berry, aged 16, a journeyman carpenter's daughter in the neighbourhood.

Thomas Noble Esq. to Miss Sally Fellows of Denham, in Buckinghamshire.

II

Mr. Molineaux, merchant in Cheapside, to Miss Sally Price of Leather-lane-Holborn, with a fortune of 50,000l.

Mr Christopher Taddy, Druggist of Pater-noster Row, to Miss Hopkins, daughter of John Hopkins Esq. of the same place and Deputy of the ward of Castle-Baynard.

At the Quaker's meeting house in Gracechurch-street, John Fothergill, nephew of Dr. Fothergill, to Miss Maria Ann Forbes.

At Kendal in Westmoreland, Captain Shearer to Miss Polly Shaw, daughter of Thomas Shaw, Esq., Alderman of that place.

"I like your Miss Bertrams exceedingly, sister," said he, as he returned from attending them to their carriage, after the said dinner visit; "they are very elegant, agreeable girls." "So they are indeed, and I am delighted to hear you say it. But you like Julia best." "Oh, yes. I like Julia best." "But do you really? for Miss Bertram is in general thought the handsomest." "So I should suppose. She has the advantage in every feature, and I prefer her countenance – but I like Julia best. Miss Bertram is certainly the handsomest, and I have found her the most agreeable, but I shall always like Julia best, because you order me."

III

At Haddington, Archibald Megget, Esq. of the Northumberland Militia, to Miss Betty Wells of Darlington

Jacob Talmage, merchant, in Goodman's Fields, to Miss Elizabeth Bennet, of the same place.

William Griffin Esq., to Miss Mary Willoughby, both of Clapham.

John Otter, Esq. of Hackney to Miss Sundelands, a young lady lately arrived from Carolina.

At Chipping Ongar, in Essex, Mr. John Wheble, Bookseller in Pater-noster-Row to Miss ____ Dore, daughter of _____Dore Esq. of Chipping Ongar.

At St. Clement Danes, Mr Nott of the Strand to Miss Elizabeth Daws of the Butcher-row.

Mr. Arnold, Tobacconist, to Mrs Bessmont; As they were going to bed the Lady was seized with an apoplectic fit and expired immediately.

James Manley, Esq., of New Bond Street to Miss Turner of Hackney, with a fortune of 15,000l.

Thomas Prescott, Esq., son of George Prescott Esq.,of Theobald's Park, in Hertfordshire, High Sheriff of that County, to Miss Frederick, daughter of Sir Charles Frederick, and niece to Lord Viscount Falmouth.

On My Wedding Gown
(A contemporary poem)

This gift, I prize all things above,
T'was given me by the man I love,
An emblem of his mind;
'Tis pure and spotless as the truth,
That fills the bosom of the youth
For whom my hand's design'd.

My Wedding Gown! O! charming thought!
With needle-work 'tis finely wrought,
And white as driven snow:
At death may we as spotless rise,
Then we'll ascend the azure skies,
And leave this world behind.

Since fate propitious has design'd
Our hands with wedlock's tie to bind,
May love our hearts unite!
While thus our minds in union move,
We'll sweeten ev'ry care with love-
'Twill make life's burden light.

Lines to Mrs. M. –On Her Marriage
(*Lady's Monthly Museum*, April 1799)

May you, Maria, hourly prove
The triumph of a virtuous mind!
May peace and pleasure crown your love,
And mutual faith your contract bind!

Blest with a husband of your choice,
'Tis your's to gild his days with joy,
To make the friend you love rejoice,
And ev'ry anxious care destroy.

Let meekness ev'ry action grace,
Nor ever think your husband wrong;
Good-humour beautify your face,
And fond affection guide your tongue.

Such are the duties of a wife,
And such are ever sure to charm;
By these you'll pass a blissful life,
Nor can the breath of slander harm.

A Young Lady's Advice to an Acquaintance
Lately Married
(*The Gentleman's Magazine*, 1763)

Dear Peggy, since the single state
You've left, and chose yourself a mate;
Since metamorphos'd to a wife,
And bliss or woe insur'd for life,
A friendly muse the way would shew,
To gain the bliss, and miss the woe.
And first of all, I must suppose
You've with mature reflection chose;
And this premis'd, I think you may
Here find to married bliss the way.
Small is the province of a wife
And narrow is her sphere of life;
Within that sphere to move aright,
Should be her principal delight:
To guide the house with prudent care,
And properly to spend and spare;
To make her husband bless the day,
He gave his liberty away:
To form the tender infant mind,
These are the tasks to wives assign'd.
Then never think domestic care
Beneath the notice of the fair,

But daily those affairs inspect,
That nought be wasted by neglect;
Be frugal, and let it be seen,
You always keep the golden mean;
Be always clean, but seldom fine;
Let decent neatness round you shine;
If once fair decency be fled,
Love soon defects the genial bed.
Not nice your house, though neat and clean,
In all things there's a proper mean;
Some of our sex mistake in this,
Too anxious some, some too remiss.
The early days of wedded life
Are oft o'ercast by childish strife;
Then be it your peculiar care,
To keep this season bright and fair,
For then's the time, by gentle art,
To fix your empire on his heart;
With kind obliging carriage strive,
To keep the lamp of love alive,
For should it through neglect expire,
No art again can light the fire.
To charm his reason, dress your mind,
Till love shall be with friendship joined.
Rais'd on that basis, 'twill endure,
From time and death itself secure.
Be sure you ne'er for power contend,
Nor try by tears to gain your end;
Sometimes the tears will cloud your eyes,
From pride and obstinacy arise.
Heaven gave to man superior sway,
Then Heaven and him at once obey.

Let sullen frowns your brows ne'er cloud;
Be always cheerful, never loud;
Let trifles never discompose
Your features, temper, or repose.
Abroad for happiness n'er roam,
True happiness resides at home;
Still make your partner easy there-
(Man finds abroad sufficient care)
If every thing at home be right,
He'll always enter with delight;
Your converse he'll prefer to all
Those cheats the world does pleasure call.
With cheerful chat his cares beguile,
And always meet him with a smile.
Should passion e'er his soul deform,
Serenely meet the bursting storm;
Never in wordy war engage,
Nor ever meet his rage with rage.
With all our sex's soft'ning art,
Recall lost reason to his heart;
Thus calm the tempest in his breast,
And sweetly smooth his soul to rest,
Be sure you ne'er arraign his sense,
Few husbands pardon that offence;
'Twill discord raise, disgust it breeds,
And hatred certainly succeeds.
Then shun, o shun, that fatal shelf,
Still think him wiser than yourself;
And if you otherwise believe,
Ne'er let him such a thought perceive,
When cares invade your partner's heart,
Bear you a sympathizing part,

And kindly claim your share of pain,
And half his troubles do sustain.
From rising morn to setting night,
To see him pleas'd be your delight
But now methinks I hear you cry,
Shall she pretend, o vanity!
To lay down rules for wedded life,
Who never was herself a wife?
I own you've ample cause to chide,
And, blushing, throw the pen aside.

A Letter to a Very Young Lady on her Marriage by Jonathan Swift (1723)

Madam,

The hurry and impertinence of receiving and paying Visits on account of your marriage, being now over, you are beginning to enter into a Course of Life, where you will want much Advice to divert you from falling into many Errors, Fopperies, and Follies to which your Sex is subject. I have always born an entire Friendship to your Father and Mother; and the person they have chosen for your Husband, hath been for some Years past my particular Favorite; I have long wished you might come together, because I hoped, that from the goodness of your Disposition, and by following the Council of wise Friends, you might in time make yourself worthy of him. Your Parents were so far in the right, that they did not produce you much into the World, whereby you avoided many wrong Steps which others have taken; and have fewer ill Impressions to be removed. But they failed, as it is generally the Case, in too much neglecting to cultivate your Mind; without which it is impossible to acquire or preserve the Friendship and Esteem of a Wise Man, who soon grows weary of acting the Lover and treating his Wife like a Mistress, but wants a reasonable Companion, and a true Friend through every Stage of his Life. It must be therefore your Business to qualify yourself for those Offices, wherein I will not fail to be your Director as long as I shall think you deserve it by letting you know how you are to act, and what you ought to avoid. And beware of despising or neglecting my Instructions, where on will depend not only your making a good figure in the World, but your own real Happiness, as well as that of the Person who ought to be the Dearest to you.

I must therefore desire you in the first place to be very slow in changing the modest behaviour of a Virgin: It is usual in young wives before they have been many Weeks married, to assume a bold, forward Look and manner of Talking, as if they intended to signify in all Companies, that they were no longer Girls, and consequently that their whole Demeanor, before they got a Husband, was all but a Countenance and Constraint upon their Nature: Whereas, I suppose, if the Votes of wise Men were gathered, a very great Majority would be in favour of those Ladies, who after they were entered into that State, rather chose to double their portion of Modesty and Reservedness.

I must likewise warn you strictly against the least degree of Fondness to your Husband before any Witness whatsoever, even before your nearest Relations, or the very Maids of your Chamber. This proceeding is so exceeding odious and disgustful to all who have either good Breeding or good Sense, that they assign two very unnamable persons for if, the one is gross Hypocrisy and the other has too bad a Name to mention. If there is any difference to be made, your Husband is the lowest Person in Company, either at Home or Abroad, and every Gentleman present has a better Claim to all marks of Civility and Distinction from you. Conceal your Esteem and Love in your own Breast and reserve your kind Looks and Language for Private hours which are so many in the Four and Twenty that they will afford time to employ a Passion as exalted as any that was even described in a French Romance.

Upon this Head I should likewise advise you to differ in Practice from those Ladies who affect abundance of Uneasiness while their Husbands are abroad, start with every Knock at the Door, and ring the Bell incessantly for the Servants to let in their Master, will not eat a bit of Dinner or Supper if the Husband happens to stay out, and receive him at his return with such a Medly of chiding and kindness, and catechising him where he has been, that a Shrew from Billingsgate would be a more easy and eligible Companion.

Of the same leaven are those Wives, who when their Husbands are gone a Journey, must have a Letter every Post, upon pain of Fits and Hystericks, and a day must be fixed for their return home without the least allowance for Business, or Sickness, or Accidents, or Weather: Upon which, I can only say that in my observation, those Ladies who were apt to make the greatest clutter upon such occasions, would liberally have paid a Messenger for bringing them news that their Husbands had broken their Necks on the Road.

You will perhaps be offended when I advise you to abate a little of that violent Passion for fine Cloaths, so predominant in your Sex. It is a little hard, that ours, for whose sake you wear them, are not admitted to be your Council: I may venture to assure you that we will make an abatement at any time of Four Pounds a yard in a Brocade, if the Ladies will but allow a suitable addition of care in the Cleanliness and Sweetness of their Persons: For, the satyrical part of mankind will needs believe, that it is not impossible, to be very fine and very filthy, and that the Capacities of a Lady are sometimes apt to fall short in cultivating Cleanliness and Finery together. I shall only add, upon so tender a subject, what a pleasant Gentleman said concerning a silly Woman of quality; that nothing could make her supportable but cutting off her Head, for his Ears were offended by her Tongue, and his Nose by her Hair and Teeth.

I am wholly at a loss how to advise you in the choice of Company, which, however, is a point of as great importance as any in your life. If your general acquaintance be among Ladies who are your equals or superiors, provided they have nothing of what is commonly called an ill Reputation, you think you are safe; and this in the style of the world will pass for Good company. Whereas I am afraid it will be hard for you to pick out one Female acquaintance in this town, from whom you will not be in manifest danger of contracting some foppery, affectation, vanity, folly, or vice. Your only safe way of conversing with them, is by a firm Resolution to proceed in your practice and behaviour directly contrary to whatever they shall say or do: And this I take to be a good General Rule, with very few exceptions. For instance, in the doctrines they usually deliver to young married women for managing their Husbands; their several accounts of their own Conduct in that particular to recommend it to your imitation; the Reflections they make upon others of their Sex for acting differently; their directions how to come off with Victory upon any dispute or quarrel you may have with your Husband; the Arts by which you may discover and practice upon his Weak sides; when to work by flattery and insinuation, when to melt him with tears, and when to engage with a high hand. In these, and a thousand other cases, it will be prudent to retain as many of their lectures in your Memory as you can, and then determine to act in full Opposition to them all.

I hope your Husband will interpose his authority to limit you in the trade of Visiting: Half a dozen fools are in all conscience as many as you should require; and it will be sufficient for you to see them twice a year: For I think the fashion does not exact, that Visits should be paid to Friends.

I advise that your company at home should consist of Men, rather than Women. To say the truth, I never knew a tolerable Woman to be [in] front of her own Sex: I confess, when both are mixt and well chosen, and put their best qualities forward, there may be an intercourse of civility and good-will; which, with the addition of some degree of sense, can make conversation or any amusement agreeable. But a Knot of Ladies, got together by themselves, is a very school of Impertinence and Detraction, and it is well if those be the worst.

Let your men acquaintance be of your Husband's choice, and not recommended to you by any She companions; because they will certainly fix a Coxcomb upon you, and it will cost you some time and pains before you can arrive at the knowledge of distinguishing such a one from a man of Sense.

Never take a Favourite waiting-maid into your Cabinet-Council, to entertain you with Histories of those Ladies whom she hath formerly served, of their Diversions and their Dresses; to insinuate how great a Fortune you brought and how little you are allowed to squander, to appeal to her from your Husband, and to be determined by her Judgment, because you are sure it will be always for you, to receive and discard Servants by her approbation or dislike; to engage you by her insinuations into misunderstandings with your best Friends; to represent all things in false colours and to be the common Emissary of Scandal.

But the Grand affair of your life will be to gain and preserve the Friendship and Esteem of your Husband. You are married to a Man of good education and learning, of an excellent understanding, and an exact taste. It is true, and it is happy for you, that these Qualities in him are adorned with great Modesty, a most amiable Sweetness of Temper, and an unusual disposition to Sobriety and Virtue: But neither Good-Nature nor Virtue will suffer him to esteem you against his Judgment; and although he is not capable of using you ill, yet you will in time grow a thing indifferent, and perhaps, contemptible; unless you can supply the loss of Youth and Beauty with more durable Qualities. You have but a very few years to be young and handsome in the eyes of the World; and as few months to be so in the eyes of a Husband who is not a Fool; for I hope you do not still dream of Charms and Raptures, which Marriage ever did, and ever will, put a sudden end to. Besides yours was a match of Prudence and common Good liking, without any mixture of that ridiculous Passion which has no Being but in Play Books and Romances.

You must therefore use all endeavours to attain to some degree of those Accomplishments which your Husband most values in other People, and for which he is most valued himself. You must improve your Mind, by closely pursuing such a Method of Study as I shall direct or approve of. You must get a collection of History and Travels which I will recommend to you, and spend some hours every day in reading them, and making extracts from them if your Memory be weak. You must invite Persons of knowledge and understanding to an acquaintance with you, by whose Conversation you may learn to correct your Taste and Judgment; and when you can bring yourself to comprehend and relish the good Sense of others; you will arrive in time to think rightly yourself, and to become a Reasonable and Agreeable Companion. This must produce in your Husband a true Rational Love and Esteem for you, which old Age will not diminish. He will have a regard for your Judgment and Opinion in matters of the greatest weight; you will be able to entertain each other without a Third Person to relieve you by finding Discourse. The endowments of your Mind will even make your Person more agreeable to him; and when you are alone, your Time will not lie heavy upon your hands for want of some trifling Amusement.

As little respect as I have for the generality of your Sex, it hath sometimes moved me with pity, to see the Lady of the House forced to withdraw immediately after Dinner, and this in Families where there is not much drinking; as if it were an established maxim, that Women are uncapable of all Conversation. In a Room where both Sexes meet, if the Men are discoursing upon any general Subject, the Ladies never think it their business to partake in what passes, but in a separate Club entertain each other with the price and choice of Lace and Silk, and what Dresses they liked or disapproved at the Church or the Play-house. And when you are among yourselves, how naturally, after the first Complements, do you apply your hands to each others Lappets and Ruffles and Mantuas, as if the whole business of your Lives, and the publick concern of the World, depended upon the Cut or Colour of your Dresses. As Divines say, that some People take more pains to be Damned, than it would cost them to be Saved; so your Sex employs more thought, memory, and application to be Fools, than would serve to make them wise and useful. When I reflect on this, I cannot conceive you to be Human Creatures, but a sort of Species hardly a degree above a Monkey; who has more diverting Tricks than any of you; is an Animal less mischievous and expensive, might in time be a tolerable Critick in Velvet and Brocade, and for ought I know wou'd equally become them.

I would have you look upon Finery as a necessary Folly, as all great Ladies did whom I have ever known; I do not desire you to be out of the fashion, but to be the last and least in it: I expect that your Dress shall be one degree lower than your Fortune can afford; and in your own heart I would wish you to be an utter Contemner of all Distinctions which a finer Petticoat can give you; because it will neither make you richer, handsomer, younger, better natur'd, more vertuous or wise, than if it hung upon a Peg.

If you are in company with Men of learning, though they happen to discourse of Arts and Sciences out of your compass, yet you will gather more advantage by listening to them, than from all the nonsense and frippery of your own Sex; but if they be Men of Breeding as well as Learning, they will seldom engage in any Conversation where you ought not to be a hearer, and in time have your part. If they talk of the Manners and Customs of the several Kingdoms of Europe, of Travels into remoter Nations, of the state of their own Country, or of the great Men and Actions of Greece and Rome; if they give their judgment upon English and French Writers, either in Verse or Prose, or of the nature and limits of Virtue and Vice, it is a shame for an English Lady not to relish such Discourses, not to improve by them, and endeavour by Reading and Information, to have her share in those Entertainments; rather than turn aside, as is the usual custom, and consult with the Woman who sits next her, about a new Cargo of Fans.

It is a little hard that not one Gentleman's daughter in a thousand should be brought to read or understand her own natural tongue, or be judge of the easiest Books that are written in it: As anyone may find, who can have the patience to hear them, when they disposed to mangle a Play or Novel, where the least word out of the common road is sure to disconcert them; and it is no wonder, when they are not so much as taught to spell in their childhood, nor can ever attain to it in their whole lives. If I advise you therefore to read aloud, more or less, every day to your Husband, if he will permit you, or to any other friend, (but not a Female one) who is able to set you right; and as for spelling, you may compass it in time by making Collections from the Books you read.

I know very well that those who are commonly called Learned Women, have lost all manner of Credit by their impertinent Talkativeness and Conceit of themselves; but there is an easy remedy for this, if you once consider, that after all the pains you may be at, you never can arrive in point of learning to the perfection of a School-boy. But the Reading I would advise you to, is only for improvement of your own good Sense, which will never fail of being Mended by Discretion. It is a wrong method, and ill choice of Books, that makes those Learned Ladies just so much worse for what they have read. And therefore it shall be my care to direct you better, a task for which I take myself to be not ill qualified; because I have spent more time, and have had more opportunities than many others, to observe and discover from what sources the various follies of Women are derived.

Pray observe how insignificant things are the common race of Ladies, when they have passed their Youth and Beauty; how contemptible they appear to the Men, and yet more contemptible to the younger part of their own Sex; and have no relief but in passing their afternoons in visits, where they are never acceptable; and their evenings at cards among each other; while the former play of the day is spent in spleen and envy or in vain endeavours to repair by art and dress the ruins of Time: Whereas I have known Ladies at Sixty, to whom all the polite part of the Court and Town paid their addresses, without any further view than that of enjoying the pleasure of their conversation.

I am ignorant of any one quality that is amiable in a Man, which is not equally so in a Woman: I do not except even Modesty and Gentleness of nature. Nor do I know one vice or folly which is not equally detestable in both. There is indeed one infirmity which is generally allowed you, I mean that of Cowardice. Yet there should seem to be something very capricious, that when Women profess their admiration for a Colonel or a Captain on account of his Valour, they should fancy it a very graceful becoming quality in themselves to be afraid of their own shadows; to scream in a Barge when the weather is calmest, or in a Coach at the Ring; to run from a Cow at a hundred yards distance; to fall into fits at the sight of a Spider, an Earwig, or a Frog. At least, if Cowardice be a sign of Cruelty, (as it is generally granted) I can hardly think it an accomplishment so desirable as to be thought worth improving by Affectation.

And as the same Virtues equally become both Sexes, so there is no quality whereby Women endeavour to distinguish themselves from Men, for which they are not just so much the worse; except that only of Reservedness; which however, as you generally manage it, is nothing else but Affectation or Hypocrisy. For as you cannot too much discountenance those of our Sex, who presume to take unbecoming liberty before you; so you ought to be wholly unconstrain'd in the company of Deserving Men, when you have had sufficient experience of their Discretion.

There is never wanting in this Town, a tribe of bold, swaggering, rattling Ladies, whose Talents pass among Coxcombs for Wit and Humour; their excellency lies in rude choquing Expressions, and what they call "running a Man down". If a gentleman in their company happens to have any Blemish in his Birth or Person, if any misfortune hath befallen his Family or himself, for which he is ashamed, they will be sure to give him broad Hints of it without any Provocation. I would recommend you to the acquaintance of a common Prostitute, rather than to that of such Termagents as these. I have often thought that no Man is obliged to suppose such Creatures to be Women; but to treat them like insolent Rascals disguised in Female Habits, who ought to be stripp'd and kick'd down Stairs.

I will add one thing although it be a little out of place, which is to desire that you will learn to value and esteem your husband for those good Qualities which he really possesseth, and not to fancy others in him which he certainly hath not. For although this latter is generally understood to be a mark of Love, yet it is indeed nothing but Affectation or ill Judgment. It is true he wants so very few Accomplishments, that you are in no great danger of erring on this side: But my Caution is occasion'd by a Lady of your Acquaintance, married to a very valuable Person, whom yet she is so unfortunate as to be always commending for those Perfections to which he can least pretend.

I can give you no advice upon the Article of Expense, only I think you ought to be well informed how much your Husband's Revenue amounts to, and to be so good a Computer as to keep within it, in that part of the Management which falls to your share; and not to put yourself in the number of those Politick Ladies, who think they gain a great Point when they have teased their Husbands to buy them a new Equipage, a lac'd Head, or a fine Petticoat, without once considering what long Scores remain unpaid to the Butcher.

I desire you will keep this Letter in your Cabinet, and often examine impartially your whole Conduct by it: And so God bless you, and make you a fair Example to your Sex, and a perpetual Comfort to your Husband and your Parents. I am, with great Truth and Affection.

Madam,

Your most faithful Friend and humble Servant

Jonathan Swift.

Hints Tending to Promote and Secure Happiness in the Married State
(*The Lady's Monthly Museum*, November 1799)

The likeliest way either to obtain a good husband or to keep one so, is to be good to yourself.

Never use a lover ill whom you design to make your husband, lest he should upbraid you with it, or return it, afterwards; and if you find, at any time, an inclination to play the tyrant, remember these two lines of truth and justice:

> Gently shall those be rul'd, who gently sway'd,
> Abject shall those obey, who haughty were obey'd.

Fanny's last feeling in the visit was disappointment – for the shawl which Edmund was quietly taking from the servant to bring and put round her shoulders was seized by Mr Crawford's quicker hand, and she was obliged to be indebted to his more prominent attention.

Battle of the Sexes

Avoid, both before and after marriage, all thoughts of managing your husband. Never endeavour to deceive or impose on his understanding, nor give him uneasiness (as some do, very foolishly) to try his temper; but treat him always before-hand, with sincerity, and afterwards with affection and respect.

Be not over-sanguine before marriage, nor promise yourself felicity without alloy; for that is impossible to be attained, in the present state of things. Consider, before-hand, that the person you are going to spend your days with, is a man, and not an angel; and if, when you come together, you discover anything in his humour or behaviour, that is not altogether so agreeable as you expect, pass it over as a human frailty: – smooth your brow, compose your temper, and try to amend it by cheerfulness and good-nature.

Remember, always, that whatever misfortunes may happen to either, they are not to be charged to the account of matrimony, but to the accidents and infirmities of human life; a burden which each has engaged to assist the other in supporting, and to which both parties are equally exposed. Therefore, instead of murmurs, reflections, and disagreement (whereby the weight is rendered abundantly more grievous) readily put your shoulder to the yoke, and make it easier to both.

Resolve every morning to be cheerful and good-natured that day; and if any accident should happen to break that resolution, suffer it not to put you out of temper with every thing besides, but especially with your husband.

Dispute not with him, be the occasion what it may; but much rather deny yourself the trivial satisfaction of having your own will, or gaining the better of an argument, than risque a quarrel, or create a heart-burning, which it is impossible to know the end of.

Be assured, a woman's power, as well as happiness, has no other foundation but her husband's esteem and love: which, consequently, it is her undoubted interest, by all means possible, to preserve and increase. Do you, therefore, study his temper, and command your own; enjoy his satisfaction with him, share and sooth his cares, and with the utmost diligence conceal his infirmities.

Read frequently, with due attention, the matrimonial service; and take care, in doing so, not to overlook the word – obey.

In your prayers, be sure to add a clause for grace to make you a good wife; and, at the same time, resolve to do your utmost endeavours towards it.

Always wear your wedding ring, for therein lies more virtue than is usually imagined; if you are ruffled unawares, assaulted with improper thoughts, or tempted in any kind against your duty, cast your eye upon it, and call to mind who gave it to you – where it was received – and what passed at that solemn time.

Let the tenderness of your conjugal love be expressed with such decency, delicacy, and prudence, as that it may appear plainly and thoroughly distinct from the designing fondness of a harlot.

Have you any concern for your own ease, or your husband's esteem? Then have a due regard to his income and circumstances in all your expences and desires; for, if necessity should follow, you run the greatest hazard of being deprived of both.

Let not many days pass together, without a serious examination how you have behaved as a wife; and if, upon reflection, you find yourself guilty of any foibles, or omissions, the best atonement is – to be exactly careful of your future conduct.

Directions for Happiness in the Married Life
(*The New Lover's Instructor*)

Let the man be all honor, the woman all love:
He as bold as a lion, she fond as the dove:
Let his arm still protect her from every disgrace,
While her gratitude's wrote in each line of her face.
In search of his fortune the husband may roam.
But returning – his wife must be ever at home.
In goodness and kindness, O let her excel!
Still as neat as a bride – not as gay as a belle;
And both, if they wish to be happy for life,
And avoid that great curse both to husband and wife,
That curse of all curses we jealousy call,
Must suppose that the passion exists not at all.
In each other confiding, their bliss is their own,
While Honor shall blend ALL THE VIRTUES IN ONE.

On the Management of Domestic Affairs
(*An Unfortunate Mother's Advice to Her Absent Daughters* by Sarah Pennington, 1761)

The management of all domestic affairs is certainly the proper business of woman, and unfashionably rustic as such an assertion may be thought, it is not beneath the dignity of any lady, however high her rank, to know how to educate her children, and to govern her servants, how to order an elegant table with economy, and to manage her whole family with prudence, regularity, and method:- If in these she is defective, whatever may be her attainments in any other kind of knowledge, she will act out of character, and, by not moving in her proper sphere, she will become rather the object of ridicule than of approbation. But, I believe, it may with truth be affirmed, that the neglect of these domestic concerns has much more frequently proceeded from an exorbitant love of diversions, from a ridiculous fondness for dress and gallantry, or from a mistaken pride that has placed such duties in a servile light, from whence they have been considered as fit only for the employment of dependants, and below the attention of a fine lady, than from too great an attachment to mental improvements. Yet, from whatsoever cause such a neglect proceeds, it is equally unjustifiable. If anything can be urged in vindication of a custom, unknown to our ancestors, which the prevalence of Fashion has made so general amongst the modern ladies, – I mean, that of committing to the care and discretionary power of different servants the sole management of their family-affairs – nothing certainly can be alleged in defence of such an ignorance, in things of this nature, as renders a lady incapable of giving proper directions on all occasions, an ignorance, which, in ever so exalted a station, will render her contemptible, even to those servants on whose understanding and fidelity she in fact becomes dependent for the regularity of her house, for the propriety, elegance, and frugality of her table, which last article is seldom regarded by such sort of people, who too frequently impose on those by whom they are too implicitly trusted. Make yourself, therefore, so thoroughly acquainted with the most proper method of conducting a family, and with the necessary expense which every article, in proportion to their number, will occasion, that you may come to a reasonable certainty of not being materially deceived without the ridiculous drudgery of following your servants constantly and meanly peeping into every obscure corner of your house. Nor is this at all difficult to attain, as it requires nothing more than an attentive observation.

It is of late, in most great families, become too much the custom to be long upon the books of every tradesman they employ. To assign a reason for this is foreign to my purpose, but I am certain it would, in general, be better, both for themselves and for the people they deal with, never to be on them at all. And what difficulty or inconvenience can arise in a well regulated family from commissioning the steward or housekeeper to pay for every thing at the time when it is brought in? – This obsolete practice, though in itself very laudable, is not at present, and perhaps never may be authorized by Fashion. However, let it be a rule with you to contract as few debts as possible, most things are to be purchased, both better in their kind, and at a lower price, by paying for them at the time of purchasing. But if, to avoid the supposed trouble of frequent trifling disbursements, you choose to have the lesser articles thrown together in a bill, let a note of the quantity and price be brought with every such parcel, – file these notes, compare them with the bill when delivered in, and let such bills be regularly paid every quarter. For it is not reasonable to expect that a tradesman should give longer credit, without making up the interest of his money by an advanced price on what he sells. And, be assured, you find it inconvenient to pay at the end of three months, that inconvenience must arise from living at too great an expence, and will consequently encrease in six months, and grow still greater at the end of the year. By making short payments you will become the sooner sensible of such a mistake, and you will find it at first more easy to retrench any supernumeraries than after having been long habituated to them.

If your house is superintended by an housekeeper, and your servants are accountable to her, let your housekeeper be accountable to yourself, and let her be entirely governed by your directions. Carefully examine her bills, and suffer no extravagances or unnecessary articles to pass unnoticed – Let these bills be brought to you every morning, what they contain will then be easily recollected without burthening your memory,- your accounts being short will be adjusted with less trouble, and with more exactness. Should you at any time have an upper servant, whose family and education were superior to that state of subjection, to which succeeding misfortunes may have reduced her, she ought to be treated with peculiar indulgence. If she has understanding enough to be conversable, and humility enough always to keep her proper distance, lessen, as much as possible every painful remembrance of former prospects, by looking on her as an humble friend, and by making her an occasional companion – But never descend to converse with those whose birth, education, and early views in life, were not superior to a state of servitude, their minds being in general suited to their station, they are apt to be intoxicated by any degree of familiarity, and to become useless and impertinent. The habit, which very many ladies have contracted, of talking to and consulting with their women, has so spoiled that lot of servants, that few of them are to be met with, who do not commence their service, by giving their unasked opinion of your person, dress or management, artfully conveyed in the too generally accepted vehicle of flattery, and, if allowed in this they will next proceed to offer their advice on any occasion that may happen to discompose or ruffle your temper. Check therefore the first appearance of such impertinence, by a reprimand sufficiently severe to prevent a repetition of it.

Give your orders in a plain, distinct manner, with good-nature, joined to a steadiness that will shew they must be punctually obeyed. Treat all your domestics with such mildness and affability that you may be served rather out of affection than from fear – Let them live happily under you, give them leisure for their own business, time for innocent recreation, and more especially for attending the public service of the church, to be instructed in their duty to God, – without which, you have no right to expect the discharge of that owing to yourself. – When wrong, tell them calmly of their faults; if they amend not, after two or three such rebukes, dismiss them – but never descend to passion and scolding, which are inconsistent with a good understanding, and beneath the dignity of a gentlewoman. Be very exact in your hours, without which there can be no order in your family, I mean those of rising, eating, & c. Require from your servants punctuality in these, and never be yourself the cause of breaking through the rules you have laid down, by deferring breakfast, putting back the dinner, or by letting it grow cold on the table, to wait your dressing, a custom by which many ladies introduce confusion, and bring their orders into neglect. Be always dressed, at least, half an hour before dinner. – Having mentioned this important article I must be allowed a little digression on the subject.

Whatever time is taken up in dress, beyond what is necessary to decency and cleanliness, may be looked upon, (to say no worse) as a vacuum in life – By decency, I mean such an habit as is suitable to your rank and fortune, – an ill-placed finery, inconsistent with either, is not ornamental but ridiculous – A compliance with Fashion, so far as to avoid the affectation of singularity, is necessary, but to run into the extreme of fashion, more especially those which are inconvenient, is the certain proof of a weak mind – Have a better opinion of yourself than to suppose you can receive any additional merit from the adventitious ornaments of dress. Leave the study of the toilet to those who are adapted to it; – I mean that insignificant set of females, whose whole life, from the cradle to the coffin, is but a varied scene of trifling, and whose intellectuals fit them not for anything beyond it. Such as these may be allowed to pass whole mornings at their looking-glass, in the important business of suiting a lot of ribands, adjusting a few curls, or determining the position of a patch – one, perhaps, of their most innocent ways of idling. But let as small a portion of your time as possible be taken up in dressing. Be always perfectly clean and neat, both in your person and clothes – equally so when alone, as in company, – look upon all beyond this as immaterial in itself, any farther than as the different ranks of mankind have made some distinction in habit, generally esteemed necessary, – and remember, that it is never the dress, however sumptuous, which reflects dignity and honour on the person – it is the rank and merit of the person that gives consequence to the dress. But to return –

It is your own steadiness and example of regularity that alone can preserve uninterrupted order in your family – If, by forgetfulness or inattention, you at any time suffer your commands to be disobeyed with impunity, your servants will grow upon such neglect into an habit of carelessness, until repeated faults (of which this is properly the source) rouse you into anger, which an even conduct would never have made necessary. Be not whimsical or capricious in your likings, approve with judgment, and condemn with reason, that acting right may be as certainly the means of obtaining your favour, as the contrary of incurring your displeasure.

From what has been said you will see, that, in order to the proper discharge of your domestic duties, it is absolutely necessary for you to have a perfect knowledge of every branch of household economy, without which, you can neither correct what is wrong, approve what is right, nor give directions with propriety. It is the want of this knowledge that reduces many a fine lady's family to a state of the utmost confusion and disorder, on the sudden removal of a managing servant, until the place is supplied by a successor of equal ability. How much out of character, how ridiculous must a mistress of a family appear, who is entirely incapable of giving practical orders on such an occasion. Let that never be **your** case – Remember, my dear, this is the only proper temporal business assigned you by Providence, and in a thing so indispensably needful, so easily attained, where so little study or application is necessary to arrive at the most commendable degree of it, the want even of perfection is almost inexcusable. Make yourself mistress of the theory, that you may be able, the more readily, to reduce it into practice. When you have a family to command, let the care of it always employ your principal attention, and let every part of it be subjected to your own inspection. If you rise early (a custom, I hope, you have not left off since you was with me), waste no unnecessary time in dressing, and if you conduct your house in a regular method, you will find many vacant hours unfilled by this material business, and no objection can be made to your employing these in such improvements of the mind as are most suitable to your genius or inclination. I believe no man of understanding will think, that, under such regulations, a woman will either make a less agreeable companion, a less useful wife, a less careful mother, or a worse mistress of a family, for all the additional knowledge her industry and application can acquire.

Love and Matrimony
(*Thoughts on the Education of Daughters with Reflections on Female Conduct in the More Important Duties of Life* by Mary Wollstonecraft, 1787)

Love

I think there is not a subject that admits so little of reasoning on as love; nor can rules be laid down that will not appear to lean too much one way or the other. Circumstances must, in a great measure, govern the conduct in this particular; yet who can be a judge in their own case? Perhaps, before they begin to consider the matter, they see through the medium of passion, and its suggestions are often mistaken for those of reason. We can no other way account for the absurd matches we every day have an opportunity of observing; for in this respect, even the most sensible men and women err. A variety of causes will occasion an attachment; an endeavour to supplant another, or being by some accident confined to the society of one person. Many have found themselves entangled in an affair of honor, who only meant to fill up the heavy hours in an amusing way, or raise jealousy in some other bosom.

It is a difficult task to write on a subject when our own passions are likely to blind us. Hurried away by our feelings, we are apt to set those things down as general maxims, which only our partial experience gives rise to. Though it is not easy to say how a person should act under the immediate influence of passion, yet they certainly have no excuse who are actuated only by vanity, and deceive by an equivocal behaviour in order to gratify it. There are quite as many male coquets as female, and they are far more pernicious pests to society, as their sphere of action is larger, and they are less exposed to the censure of the world. A smothered sigh, downcast look, and the many other little arts which are played off, may give extreme pain to a sincere, artless woman, though she cannot resent, or complain of, the injury. This kind of trifling, I think, much more inexcusable than inconstancy; and why it is so, appears so obvious, I need not point it out.

People of sense and reflection are most apt to have violent and constant passions, and to be preyed on by them. Neither can they, for the sake of present pleasure, bear to act in such a manner, as that the retrospect should fill them with confusion and regret. Perhaps a delicate mind is not susceptible of a greater degree of misery, putting guilt out of the question, than what must arise from the consciousness of loving a person whom their reason does not approve. This, I am persuaded, has often been the case; and the passion must either be rooted out, or the continual allowances and excuses that are made will hurt the mind, and lessen the respect for virtue. Love, unsupported by esteem, must soon expire, or lead to depravity; as, on the contrary, when a worthy person is the object, it is the greatest incentive to improvement, and has the best effect on the manners and temper. We should always try to fix in our minds the rational grounds we have for loving a person, that we may be able to recollect them when we feel disgust or resentment; we should then habitually practice forbearance, and the many petty disputes which interrupt domestic peace would be avoided. A woman cannot reasonably be unhappy, if she is attached to a man of sense and goodness, though he may not be all she could wish.

I am very far from thinking love irresistible, and not to be conquered. "If weak women go astray," it is they, and not the stars, that are to be blamed. A resolute endeavour will almost always overcome difficulties. I knew a woman very early in life warmly attached to an agreeable man, yet she saw his faults; his principles were unfixed, and his prodigal turn would have obliged her to have restrained every benevolent emotion of her heart. She exerted her influence to improve him, but in vain did she for years try to do it. Convinced of the impossibility, she determined not to marry him, though she was forced to encounter poverty and its attendants.

It is too universal a maxim with novelists, that love is felt but once; though it appears to me, that the heart which is capable of receiving an impression at all, and can distinguish, will turn to a new object when the first is found unworthy. I am convinced it is practicable, when a respect for goodness has the first place in the mind, and notions of perfection are not affixed to constancy. Many ladies are delicately miserable, and imagine that they are lamenting the loss of a lover, when they are full of self-applause, and reflections on their own superior refinement. Painful feelings are prolonged beyond their natural course, to gratify our desire of appearing heroines, and we deceive ourselves as well as others. When any sudden stroke of fate deprives us of those we love, we may not readily get the better of the blow; but when we find we have been led astray by our passions, and that it was our own imaginations which gave the high colouring to the picture, we may be certain time will drive it out of our minds. For we cannot often think of our folly without being displeased with ourselves, and such reflections are quickly banished. Habit and duty will co-operate, and religion may overcome what reason has in vain combated with; but refinement and romance are often confounded, and sensibility, which occasions this kind of inconstancy, is supposed to have the contrary effect.

Nothing can more tend to destroy peace of mind, than platonic attachments. They are begun in false refinement, and frequently end in sorrow, if not in guilt. The two extremes often meet, and virtue carried to excess will sometimes lead to the opposite vice. Not that I mean to insinuate that there is no such thing as friendship between persons of different sexes; I am convinced of the contrary. I only mean to observe, that if a woman's heart is disengaged, she should not give way to a pleasing delusion, and imagine she will be satisfied with the friendship of a man she admires and prefers to the rest of the world. The heart is very treacherous, and if we do not guard its first emotions, we shall not afterwards be able to prevent its sighing for impossibilities. If there are any insuperable bars to an union in the common way, try to dismiss the dangerous tenderness, or it will undermine your comfort, and betray you into many errors. To attempt to raise ourselves above human beings is ridiculous; we cannot extirpate our passions, nor is it necessary that we should, though it may be wise sometimes not to stray too near a precipice, lest we fall over before we are aware. We cannot avoid much vexation and sorrow, if we are ever so prudent; it is then the part of wisdom to enjoy those gleams of sunshine which do not endanger our innocence, or lead to repentance. Love gilds all the prospects of life, and though it cannot always exclude apathy, it makes many cares appear trifling. Dean Swift hated the world, and only loved particular persons; yet pride rivalled them. A foolish wish of rising superior to the common wants and desires of the human species made him singular, but not respectable. He sacrificed an amiable woman to his caprice, and made those shun his company who would have been entertained and improved by his conversation, had he loved anyone as well as himself. Universal benevolence is the first duty, and we should be careful not to let any passion so engross our thoughts, as to prevent our practising it. After all the dreams of rapture,

211

earthly pleasures will not fill the mind, or support it when they have not the sanction of reason, or are too much depended on. The tumult of passion will subside, and even the pangs of disappointment cease to be felt. But for the wicked there is a worm that never dies – a guilty conscience. While that calm satisfaction which resignation produces, which cannot be described, but may be attained, in some degree, by those who try to keep in the strait, though thorny path which leads to bliss, shall sanctify the sorrows, and dignify the character of virtue.

Matrimony

Early marriages are, in my opinion, a stop to improvement. If we were born only "to draw nutrition, propagate and rot," the sooner the end of creation was answered the better; but as women are here allowed to have souls, the soul ought to be attended to. In youth a woman endeavours to please the other sex, in order, generally speaking, to get married, and this endeavour calls forth all her powers. If she has had a tolerable education, the foundation only is laid, for the mind does not soon arrive at maturity, and should not be engrossed by domestic cares before any habits are fixed. The passions also have too much influence over the judgment to suffer it to direct her in this most important affair; and many women, I am persuaded, marry a man before they are twenty, whom they would have rejected some years after. Very frequently, when the education has been neglected, the mind improves itself, if it has leisure for reflection, and experience to reflect on; but how can this happen when they are forced to act before they have had time to think, or find that they are unhappily married? Nay, should they be so fortunate as to get a good husband, they will not set a proper value on him; he will be found much inferior to the lovers described in novels, and their want of knowledge makes them frequently disgusted with the man, when the fault is in human nature.

When a woman's mind has gained some strength, she will in all probability pay more attention to her actions than a girl can be expected to do; and if she thinks seriously, she will chuse for a companion a man of principle; and this perhaps young people do not sufficiently attend to, or see the necessity of doing. A woman of feeling must be very much hurt if she is obliged to keep her children out of their father's company, that their morals may not be injured by his conversation; and besides, the whole arduous task of education devolves on her, and in such a case it is not very practicable. Attention to the education of children must be irksome, when life appears to have so many charms, and its pleasures are not found fallacious. Many are but just returned from a boarding-school, when they are placed at the head of a family, and how fit they are to manage it, I leave the judicious to judge. Can they improve a child's understanding, when they are scarcely out of the state of childhood themselves?

Dignity of manners, too, and proper reserve are often wanting. The constant attendant on too much familiarity is contempt. Women are often before marriage prudish, and afterwards they think they may innocently give way to fondness, and overwhelm the poor man with it. They think they have a legal right to his affections, and grow remiss in their endeavours to please. There are a thousand nameless decencies which good sense gives rise to, and artless proofs of regard which flow from the heart, and will reach it, if it is not depraved. It has ever occurred to me, that it was sufficient for a woman to receive caresses, and not bestow them. She ought to distinguish between fondness and tenderness. The latter is the sweetest cordial of life; but, like all other cordials, should be reserved for particular occasions; to exhilarate the spirits, when depressed by sickness, or lost in sorrow. Sensibility will best instruct. Some delicacies can never be pointed out or described, though they sink deep into the heart, and render the hours of distress supportable.

A woman should have so proper a pride, as not easily to forget a deliberate affront; though she must not too hastily resent any little coolness. We cannot always feel alike, and all are subject to changes of temper without an adequate cause.

Reason must often be called in to fill up the vacuums of life; but too many of our sex suffer theirs to lie dormant. A little ridicule and smart turn of expression, often confutes without convincing; and tricks are played off to raise tenderness, even while they are forfeiting esteem.

Women are said to be the weaker vessel, and many are the miseries which this weakness brings on them. Men have in some respects very much the advantage. If they have a tolerable understanding, it has a chance to be cultivated. They are forced to see human nature as it is, and are not left to dwell on the pictures of their own imaginations. Nothing, I am sure, calls forth the faculties so much as the being obliged to struggle with the world; and this is not a woman's province in a married state. Her sphere of action is not large, and if she is not taught to look into her own heart, how trivial are her occupations and pursuits! What little arts engross and narrow her mind! "Cunning fills up the mighty void of sense," and cares, which do not improve the heart or understanding, take up her attention. Of course, she falls a prey to childish anger, and silly capricious humors, which render her rather insignificant than vicious.

In a comfortable situation, a cultivated mind is necessary to render a woman contented; and in a miserable one, it is her only consolation. A sensible, delicate woman, who by some strange accident, or mistake, is joined to a fool or a brute, must be wretched beyond all names of wretchedness, if her views are confined to the present scene. Of what importance, then, is intellectual improvement, when our comfort here, and happiness hereafter, depend upon it.

Principles of religion should be fixed, and the mind not left to fluctuate in the time of distress, when it can receive succour from no other quarter. The conviction that everything is working for our good will scarcely produce resignation, when we are deprived of our dearest hopes. How they can be satisfied, who have not this conviction, I cannot conceive; I rather think they will turn to some worldly support, and fall into folly, if not vice. For a little refinement only leads a woman into the wilds of romance, if she is not religious; nay, more, there is no true sentiment without it, nor perhaps any other effectual check to the passions.

Of the Marriage-State : Directing Women how to behave themselves towards their Husbands, Children, Servants and Relations, in all Affairs, both Abroad and at Home.
(*The Whole Duty of a Woman by a Lady*, 1695)

Having led you through the Virgin State I now bring you to a Change of Condition, to that which is called a Marriage State, which is Launching into a wide Ocean, comparable to the former. For here, as you Marry the Person, so do you his Obligations, and wherever he, by Ties of Nature or Alliance, owes a Reverence or Kindness, you are no less a Debtor; your Marriage is an Adoption into his Family and therefore you are to pay to every branch of it, whatever their Stations

His happiness in knowing himself to have been so long the beloved of such a heart must been great enough to warrant any strength of language in which he could clothe it to her or to himself; it must have been a delightful happiness. But there was happiness elsewhere which no description can reach. Let no one presume to give the feelings of a young woman on receiving the assurance of that affection of which she has scarcely allowed herself to entertain a hope.

respectively require. But this State, for Brevity sake, I will reduce under three Heads, or Considerations viz. A Wife, a Mother and a Mistress.

1. A Wife has her Duty to observe in several respects, as it relates,

1. To her Husband's Person
2. To his Reputation
3. To his Fortune
4. To his Friends and Relations

1. To his Person, in the first Place is owing the Debt of Love, a prime Article in the Marriage Vow; and indeed that is the most Essential Requisite, for without it there is nothing in Marriage comfortable, and indeed, where it is wanting, Marriage is only an Empty Name, or what is worse, Tyranny on the Husband's Part, and Slavery on the Wife's; unless by struggling she gets Dominion, and then it goes worse. Therefore as it is necessary to bring a large degree of Love to this State, so it is no less to maintain and improve it in it. This is that which Facilitates all other Duties of Marriage. It must therefore [being entered into it] be your chief Care, and Study to preserve this Flame, and like the Vestal Fire, it may never go out. And to that end, carefully to guard it from all those Things that are apt to extinguish it, as Frowardness, all little Perverseness of Humour and Morose Behaviour, which by taking off from the Delight and Complacence of Conversation, will by Degrees wear out the Kindness, and overturn the Empire of Love.

Above all Things avoid Jealousie, and that even puts out the Snuff of Love's Torch, as well as the Flame, embitters all the sweets of Life, and though it be held to be the Child of Love, yet like the Vipers Ungrateful Blood, it destroys its Parent in its Birth, and as you desire to live without the greatest Torture of Life in avoiding it yourself, as not giving heed to Fables, or idle Reports, nay nor to very probable ones, if you love your own Ease and Quiet: So on your Part, be Nicely careful to give your Husband no Umbrage or Colour for it, though in an innocent Freedom and Discourse or Conversation, where he seems to dislike of it, for this is a Fire that Kindles with a Spark, and soon bursts out into a violent Flame, hardly, if ever, to be Extinguished.

2. You must be careful of his good Name and Reputation, for therein your own Interest is mainly concerned and if Blots fasten on him, the Censorious World will not spare to Stain you, his Reproach will refund upon you, and you are liable to share with him in that, as well as in other Things, for if he suffers in that, you cannot escape.

3. If Crosses and Misfortunes should decline your Fortune, and Prosperity take her flight, Love must not Lessen or decline with it, but rather shine in a higher Perfection, that it may be evident you loved his Person more than his Wealth: For indeed, herein the vertue of a Wife is more eminently shewn, viz. In the Tryal of her Patience and Suffering, when in Prosperity it could not be so easily distinguished, where no Probations offer, our Duties though Duties incumbent, are not well understood, especially to others, tho' they are performed in a great measure.

If a Husband prove not what you expected in relation to Temper and good Humour, yet by a wise Use of every Thing, he may, by degrees, be turned to be very Supportive, which Prudence neglected, might in Time beget an Aversion. Consider then, since the greater Share of Reason is bestowed

on Man, as the Lawgiver, our Sex is the better prepared for the
Compliance that is necessary for better Performance of those
Duties, that seem to be most properly Assigned to it, and
although this may seem something unpleasing at first, upon
Examination it will be found, that Nature is so far from being
unjust to us, that She is partial on our side, and for the seeming
Injustice, has made large amends for the other Advantage the
Right of complaining by that Means being come over to us,
it is in our Power, not only to free ourselves, but to subdue
our Master, and without Violence throw both their Natural
and Legal Authority at our Feet. The Sexes are made of
Different Tempers, that the Defects may be better supplied
by mutual Assistance. Our Sex wants the others Reason for
our Conduct, and their Strength for our Protection. Theirs
want our Gentleness to soften and Entertain them, our Looks
have more Strength than their Laws; there is more Power
in our Tears, than in their Arguments, and therefore Things
prudently managed, will by degrees bring over a Husband to
see his Errors, and by acknowledging his Failings, take Care
for the future to mend them, but then the Wife's Gentleness
and Vertues must be the Mirror, wherein he must see the
Deformity of his Irregularities.

4. Something more must be said in this Point in the Conduct
of your Behaviour to his Relations and Friends. For many
Times a neglect or slight regard of them, make wide Breaches
in a Family : You may be sure they will not fail to resent
any sensible Disrespect and Complaints; or, will not always
fail to stir up your Husband's Anger against you, especially
when he concludes himself injur'd by it, and therefore you
must consider how to carry yourself even with them. For the
Family into which you are engrafted will generally be apt to

expect that, like a Stranger in a Foreign Country, you should in a great Measure conform to their Methods if they are of any considerable Degree, and not bring in a new Model, by your own Authority. And therefore that you may with the less Difficulty afterwards give your Directions, you ought to take them first from your Husband's Friends, if an Opportunity offers, gain them by early applying to them, and they will be so satisfied, that as nothing is more thankful than Pride, when it is complyed with, that they will strive which of them shall most recommend to you, and when they contribute to your taking firm Root in your Husband's good Opinion, you will have no less Dependance on theirs, tho' you ought not to neglect any reasonable Means of preserving it. Consider, where a Husband is governed as it were by his Friends, he is easily inflamed by them, and he that is not so, will notwithstanding for his own sake expect to have them considered, it is easily improved to a point of Honour in a Husband, not to have his Relations neglected. And nothing is found more dangerous in this kind, than to raise an Objection grounded on Pride, it is the most stubborn and lasting Passion we are subjected to, and where it begins a War it is very hard to make a secure Peace. Therefore use them well and be well with them, and they will not fail to support you in your Husband's Love; and then if Discontents arise, it is your own Fault.

The next Thing I am to lay down in the State of Marriage, is, The office and Duty of a Mother: And this may be branch'd into many Severals; but many of them being not very significant, I shall only reduce them under two Heads, viz.

Love and Care. A Mother is a title of so much Tenderness, that we find it borrowed by our common Dialect to express the tenderest of all kindness. So that Nature seems sufficient to have secured the Love of a Mother, towards the Fruit of her Womb, without the Aid of any positive Law, unless where Monsters in Wickedness, and that very seldom, give contrary Precedents, to the Blot of Name, Abhorrence, and lasting Infamy. The Love of a Parent, however the Children may afterwards prove, ought and indeed naturally is descending, all Things move most violently downwards. So that whereas that of Children to their Parents commonly needs a Spur, this of the Mother frequently requires a Bridle, who by Strength of Feminine Passion, usually exceeds the Father.

Therefore to regulate this Affection, you are diligently to advert to these two Rules.

1. That you hurt not yourself by this Excess of Love
2. That you hurt not your Children

Of the first you are in danger, if you suffer that Humane Affection to swell beyond its Banks, so as to come in any competition with the Divine, for then you dishonour God, by making an Idol of your Child; and for this cause Covetousness is in one Sense called Idolatry, because what anyone sets his or her Affections upon entirely, he or she is supposed to Idolize, and frame it in their Imaginations as a God, though, in Reality, it be nothing so, and I cannot but fear God, upon this Account, has been displeased with too many Mothers, and sent them Afflictions even to Humbling, by (as in some sense I may term it) untimely taking from them those Children they Idolize, to the prejudice of his Honour, and even of their own Souls. For indeed every Thing is so accounted, That Rivals the Love of God in our Hearts, and she who owns the Title of a Jealous God, cannot be reasonably thought to bear it, without one way or other Punishing us.

By this however, I do not mean you should follow the Example of those, who immoderately Love their own Pleasure, and do not in the least Regard their Children (which God has given them as immediate Blessings) looking on them as a Clog to keep them within Doors: and think their Adverting to them will hinder their gadding Abroad, turning them over for that Reason, which indeed is but a very slender one) to the Care of a Nurse, or a Maid, whilst perhaps a Dog or Monkey is thought worth their own Attendance. This is so much in the Extream of the other Side, and seems beyond the Bowels of a Motherly Tenderness.

But as to the former Matter, whether Beautiful or Homely, make no difference in your Maternal Care and Affection because they proceeded from you, and it is not in the Power of the Infant to Form itself; but it is formed in the Womb by the wonderful Working of Almighty God, and Shaped as he pleases. And many Times to mend the Defect, A Distorted Body Rumpled in the Cells of Nature, is endowed with a Beautiful Soul, when that cast in a fairer Mould, to outward Appearance, is an Idiot, or like a Picture, only representing a Proportion and Stature to the Eye, without Intellectual Faculties to make it what it Represents.

In this case a Mother that pretends Vertue must make no Difference, but divide her Affections equally, yet so, that they may be Moderate and not infringe on that Love she owes her Maker. Where the Acts of the Soul are considered there must be no Competitor in Affection with the Almighty, but he must be all in all, as to Divine Love, for he is the only unlimited Object of it, and if you exceed in this, you hurt yourself, and bring on his Wrath in Punishment here, and if not repented of, perhaps Eternally hereafter.

Secondly, As I have already hinted, you hurt your Children in not bringing them up in due Obedience and respect towards you; whereas, when you generally Dote upon all, or more particularly on One, it cannot be brought to pass, for then, thro' want of that Strict Government, which in many Cases is required, and an Over-indulgence will not permit you to exercise yourself, nor you others to do it, they will without a wonderful Providence, grow Stubborn and Headstrong, as they grow in Years. The only justifiable Ground of Partiality, if you single out any of the Number of your Children as a Favourite, must be Vertue and this must only extend to provoke a Vertuous Emulation in the Rest, and then you must so manage it, as to Evidence it is no Inequality in your own Inclination, but meerly the Force of the others Deserts, not the Person of your Child, but the Goodness that Biasses you, and when Vertue is known to be the only Ingratiating Quality, the rest may labour perhaps to become yours and God's Favourites. Therefore shew them early an Example of Piety, in your own Life and Conversation. And in the Decorum of your Family, keep them out of the hearing of Vain Words, or any Thing that may tend to violate their tender Years, by which they are too apt to take deeply the first Impression of Words or Actions, not by Time so easily Obliterated as may be imagined. And in Matters of the Vertuous Education of your Children, you are not only Accountable to yourself but God. He seems to say to you, as King Pharoah's Daughter did to the Mother of Moses "Take this Child and Nurse it for me." The end for which he gives them, is, that they should be brought up in his Fear, that they may live, grow up, and die in his Favour. And then you may have the Comfort of meeting them again in an endless Eternity of Blessedness, never more to be Separated. And this will certainly add to those Joys, that

in themselves are very Excellent – That you have brought
forth, and trained up Children to live and reign with Christ in
his Kingdom of Glory.

The best Way of approving your Love towards them is,
by the Duty of Care. Without this, all the most Passionate
Raptures of Kindness are but an Airy Apparition, a Fantastical
Scene, and will no more advantage a Child, than a Picture of
Food will nourish if. Nor is this Care a Temporary, Momentary
Duty, but it must be taken through the several Stages of
Infancy, Childhood and Youth.

The first of these is a Season only for those Cares that
concern the Bodies of your Children. Providing for their careful
Attendance and all other Things conducing to strengthen their
Constitutions, laying a Foundation for future Health and
Vigour, which is your Interest not only upon the Body, but
upon an Intellectual Account: The good Temperature of the
Body being a great Aid towards the free Operation of the
Mind. But this Health is not always the Consequent of a Nice
Breeding, for that many times overthrows it, when inuring
them to moderate Hardships, seldom fails of giving a strong
and healthful Constitution. Too much Feeding and Delicacies
breed Humours, by reason of a weak Digestion to which most
Children in their Infancy are subject, and the super-abundance
of Humours breeding Diseases, which often become Habitual,
or too sadly end in Early Death, when moderate Feeding, and
exposing them to the fresh Air abroad, and not Mewing, or
as it were Stifling them in a Nursery, gives 'em Strength and
Refreshment; for when Nature is not over-loaded, she makes
a due Digestion, which turns to sweet and wholesome Blood,
and kindly Humours, but being over-loaded or oppressed,
she is almost Suffocated, and cannot exercise her Function to
proper Advantages: And as for a free breathing Air, refined

from Damps and Grossness, it rarifies the Lungs and Vital Spirits, and is the great Refresher of Life. But of these I shall speak more, when I come to treat of Ordering Children, as to their Health in Diet and Physical Matters.

Secondly, when they are past Infancy, if you Dote, so as to hoodwink yourself, because you will not see their Faults, or Manacle your hands that you cannot Chastise them, then it will be imputed your fault, if their Vices grow up with them, and you will find little Comfort of them in the End, tho' you promise yourself never so much in lieu of your Kindness towards them. For when the Mother's Affections are Unbridled the Child's will be so too. The Wise Man, in this case, gives you better Advice, viz. Bow down the Neck of a Child from its Youth, that is, bring it up to strict Rules of Vertue, and put a Bridle on its stubborn Inclinations, and so when it grows up, it will Bless you, not only as its Parent but Preserver; and secure to it the future happiness of Life. For if you permit them to run on in their own vain Devices, in hopes Time may alter it, by making them see their Folly and grow Wiser, you will be too often miserably Mistaken; for as their Joynts knit and gather Strength, so do their ill Habits, till at last they are confirmed in an Obstinacy, and by that means you set them in a perfect Opposition to the Pattern they should Imitate. For as Christ's Childhood increased in Wisdom, and the Divine Favour. Luke 2. So will theirs in all those Provoking Follies, which may avert both the Love of God and Man, and then, alas, what Recompense can the little Blandishments and Caresses of a Mother make her Children for such important and inestimable Mischief. So that if you would be kind, you must temper your Indulgence with a prudent severity, or else you eminently Violate this second Rule, by which you should Regulate your Love, and so do that to them, which

Jacob feared from his Father Gen. 27. Bring a Curse upon them, and not a Blessing.

Thirdly, In the next Period of their time when they are arrived at Years of Reason and Growth, then you may be more familiar with them, they having been seasoned to know their Distance and Duty. Allow them such a kind yet Motherly Freedom, that they may have a Complaisancy in your Conversation, and not be tempted to seek it amongst their Inferiors. That the Belief of your Kindness may supplant the Pretensions of those mean Sycophants, who by little Flatteries, endeavour to screw themselves into their good Opinion, and become their Confidents, than which, especially to Daughters, there is nothing more Mischievous, in teaching them Disobedience, and rendering them Mutinous against their Parents, by buzzing into their Ears the wild Notions of unbounded Liberty and Freedom, which Lectures they should not so soon be trusted withal. Besides, those Intimacies are often Introductions to worse, many scandalous Amours, and unequal Matches have had their Rise from them. It must therefore be your Business to prevent all such pernicious Leagues in pre-ingaging them in more safe Familiarities, either with yourself, or some others, of whose Vertues you have reason to be Confident.

But the most Infallible Security against this, and all other Mischiefs, is to bring them to an Intimacy and Conversation with their Maker, by fixing a true Sense of Religion in their Souls, for if that can effectually be done, it will Supersede all other Expedients. For if they duly consider they are always in God's Presence they will want no other Inspector, nor much need Monitors, if they seriously attend to the Advice of their own Conscience. Neither will it tend only to the securing of their Innocency, but their Reputation, it being one part of the Christian Law to Abstain from all Appearances of Evil, 1 Thess.5.22. To do things that are of good Report, Phil. 4.8. So that Piety is the only compleat Armour, to defend at once their Vertue and their Fame. And it is extreamly necessary they should be furnished with it, at this Age especially.

It is sad to be considered indeed, that some Mothers neglect this most important Concern in their Daughters, tho' nicely Curious in their other Parts of Breeding. They give them Civil Accomplishments but no Christian, those are excluded by them out of the Scheme of Education, and by that means be under the Prejudice of being not only Unnecessary, but Ungenteel, below the regard of a Person of Quality. I suppose this is often increased by a little vanity they have in seeing them excel in some of those Exterior Qualities, which may recommend them to the Humour of the World, upon the Improving whereof they are so Intent, that more material things are overlook'd. And so this part of the Business, or Duty of a Wife, I shall conclude, in advising you to be careful in Placing or Bestowing your Children in the World, either in Marriage or Business, that they may flourish in Piety and Wealth, and be the lasting Comforts of your Life.

A Mistress is another Obligation Incumbent on you when Marry'd, if you live in any Quality and Repute in the World; for in such a Case, the Inspection of the Family is usually your Province; for tho' you are not Supreme there, yet you are to improve your delegated Authority to the Advantage of them under it, and your more Constant Residence gives you more Opportunities of it, than the frequent Avocations of your Husband will perhaps allow him. St Paul sets this as the Calling and Indispensable Duty of a Married Woman. That she guide the House 1 Tim.5.14. Not thinking it a Point of Greatness to remit the Management of all Domestick Concerns to a Mercenary Housekeeper.

Now, as to all your well-guiding of your House, I know no better Rule, than that you endeavour to make all that are yours to be God's Servants also; This will secure you of all those intermedial Qualifications in them, in which your Secular Interest is concerned, their own Consciences being the best Spy you can set upon them, as to their Truth and Fidelity, and also the best Spur to Industry and Diligence.

A Christian Family should be the Epitome of a Church. It is not only the Duty, but Interest, of all that have Families, to keep up the Esteem and Practice of Religion in them. It was one of the greatest Endearments of Abraham to God, That he would command his Household to keep the Way of the Lord, Gen. 18.19. And Joshua undertakes no less for the Piety of his House than himself, "As for me" says he," and my House, we will serve the Lord" Job 24.15. But when Piety is planted in a Family, it will soon wither, if it be not kept in Vigour by Discipline. This you must promote by your own Example to your Servants, calling upon them to mind their Duty to God; and observe they do not Neglect it, or do it Hypocritically, for Form and Compliance only, which may be discerned in their Conversations elsewhere.

You must not fall into Mistakes of thinking because they receive Wages, and are so inferior to you, they are therefore beneath your Care, to know how to Manage them. They are the moving Engines of your Family, and let your Directions be never so Faultless, yet if they stop, or move Irregular, the whole Order of the House will be at a stand, or discomposed. Besides, the Inequality which is between you, must not make you forget, that Nature maketh no such Distinction. But that Servants ought at least to be look'd upon as humble Friends;

and that Usage, and returns of Kindness, are as much due to those that deserve it, as their Services due to you, when you require it. A foolish Haughtiness in the Stile of Speaking, or in the Manner of Commanding them, is in itself very unseemly, and frequently begets Aversion in them, of which the least ill Effect to be expected, is, That they will be Slow and Careless in all you Enjoyn them: And by Experience you will find it True, that you will be so much the more Obeyed, as you are the less Imperious.

Be not too hasty in giving your orders, nor too angry when they are not altogether observed; much less be not Loud, or appear too much Disturbed. An evenness in distinguishing when they do well or ill, will make them move by a Rule, and without Noise, and will the better set out your Skill in Conducting Matters with Ease and Silence. Let there be well chosen Houshold Affairs, which may be distinguish'd from the rest of your Time, that the necessary Cares may come in their proper Place, without any Influence upon your good Humour, or interruption to other Things. By those Methods you will put yourself into a Condition of being valued by your Servants, and you need not doubt, but their Obedience will Naturally follow.

The Art of laying out your Money Wisely, must be one of your greatest Cares; it is not attained without considerable Thought; and it is yet more difficult in the case of a Wife, who is accountable to her husband for her Mistakes in it. In this therefore you are to keep a Mean, between the two Extreams of Profuseness and Niggardly Temper, and if you cannot hold the Balance even, let it incline rather towards the Liberal side, as more suitable to your Quality, and less subject to Reproach. A little Money mispent is sooner recovered, than the Credit which is lost by having it unhandsomely saved, and a prudent Husband will less forgive a shameful Piece of Parsimony, than a little Extravagancy if it be not too often repeated. Give no just Cause to the meanest Servant you entertain, to complain of the Want of any Thing that is Necessary. Above all fix your Thoughts as an unchangeable Maxim, that nothing is truly fine but what is fit, and that just what is proper for your Circumstances, of their several Kinds is much finer than all you can add to it: For those that break through these Bounds, launch into the wide Sea of Extravagancy; and then every Thing will become Necessary, because they have a Mind to it; not so properly, because it is fit, but because some body has it. This Lady's Logick sets Reason with its Heels upwards, by carrying the Rule from Things to Persons, and appealing from what is Right, to every Fool that is in the Wrong. Remember That Children and Fools want every Thing that they see, because they have not Wit to distinguish what is reasonably Necessary: And therefore there is no stronger Evidence of a crazy Understanding, than making too large a Catalogue of Things Necessary, when indeed there are so very few that have a Right to be placed in it. Let your Judgment first make a Tryal of every Thing, before you allow it a Place in your Desire, else your Husband may conceive it as necessary to deny, as it is for you to crave whatever is Unreasonable; and if you should too often give him that Advantage, 'tis ten to one often but the Habit of Refusing, may reach to things that are not unfit for you.

ESSAYS ADDRESSED TO YOUNG
MARRIED WOMEN
By Elizabeth Griffith (1782)

INTRODUCTION

Almost every moral Writer or Essayist that I have happened to meet with, from the days of Solomon to the present aera, have complained of the profligacy and degeneracy of their Times.

"And so, there she had sat, without an idea of anything in the world, full ten minutes, perhaps – when, all of a sudden, who should come in – to be sure it was so very odd! – but they always dealt at Ford's – who should come in but Elizabeth Martin and her brother! Dear Miss Woodhouse ! – only think. I thought I should have fainted. I did not know what to do. I was sitting near the door – Elizabeth saw me directly; but he did not; he was busy with the umbrella."

From hence we are led to believe, that folly and vice have been equally prevalent in all ages, and that there is no such period to be found in the annals of Human Nature, as that Golden Age in which Wisdom and Virtue dwelt with Men.

That perfection is not the lot of mortals, I readily admit, and cannot therefore presume to point out the exact modes of any particular period of time as objects of general imitation; but without venturing to oppose my slight opinion against the common and willingly-received adage, that the world is just as good as it was a thousand years ago, I will pronounce, that though Virtue and Vice may have travelled progressively upon the same scale since the Creation to this day, the influence of Folly, and her inseparable companions Vanity and Dissipation, have, within the present century, been extended in Britain to a degree not only unknown to, but inconceivable by, our Ancestors.

The chief causes of this sad effect, we are told, originate in the improper plan of education which has been adopted for our young Ladies. But as new and useful lights have been thrown upon this subject by abler pens than mine, particularly by those excellent and elegant Writers Mrs. Chapone and Miss More, I shall not dwell upon it; but mean humbly to offer my sentiments to those of my sex who, having passed through the restraints necessarily imposed on youth, are ready to launch into the tempestuous ocean of life, without any chart to sail by but their native innocence and unsuspecting chearfulness.

While they preserve the first, they will not strike against the rock most fatal to their peace; but grant they should escape that imminent danger, there are a thousand hidden shoals within this stormy sea, where female happiness may suffer wreck. From these it is my most earnest wish to save them, and send them floating down the stream of Time loaded with days and honour.

As it is generally supposed that a thorough knowledge of the art we mean to teach is indispensably necessary in every science, the Author of the following Essays, with the truest gratitude to the Almighty for such an inestimable blessing, presumes to hope, that after thirty years of uninterrupted happiness in the marriage-state, she may be deemed qualified, at least as far as experience can direct, to speak upon the most interesting of all earthly subjects to those who are but entering on that state of probation, wherein a strict adherence to its delightful duties must lead to the final reward of happiness here and hereafter.

RELIGION

From the time that a Woman enters into the holy and honourable state of matrimony, she becomes accountable for her conduct both towards God and Man. Separated from the fostering care of tender and indulgent parents, who have hitherto directed her footsteps in the way that she should walk, and left to chuse her path amidst the stormy or the flowery way, where shall she find a clue to direct her inexperience through the labyrinth that now lies before her? One unerring guide remains, which if she truly seeks, "his word will be a lanthorn to her feet, and a light unto her paths," and when her father and her mother forsake her, "he will take her up."

As the spring to the year, so is youth to the soul, the season of blooming virtue: without blossoms, there can be no fruit, and the barren mind that is not early imbued with the knowledge of the love of God, which alone constitutes our happiness here, and our hopes hereafter, will seek in vain for the delight it yields in those maturer days, when worldly cares and disappointments have soured the natural benevolence of the heart, and rendered it callous to the refined feelings of sensibility.

Zeal without knowledge is the parent of bigotry; and bigotry is too often the adopted religion of wrinkles and grey hairs. From hence it sometimes happens, that devotion assumes the mask of austerity, which, by concealing the beauty of holiness, must rather deter than invite the inexperienced mind from entering into that service "which is perfect freedom, whose ways are ways of pleasantness, and whose paths are those of peace."

But whilst the blessings and pleasures of youth flow around us, the heart must naturally be expanded with gratitude; gratitude produces praise, and praise is surely the most acceptable sacrifice that a human creature can offer to the great Author of good. But, alas, surrounded by the delights of life, we too frequently become forgetful of the source from whence they are derived; and whilst we are indulging all our appetites in the delicious stream of happiness, it becomes impregnated with the qualities of Lethé, and renders us unmindful of its fountain.

Let then the sensible and innocent Bride "remember her Creator in the days of her youth, while the evil days come not, nor the years draw nigh when she shall say I have no pleasure in them." [Ecclesiastes 10 v.1] Doctor Young says, "The whole creation cannot furnish a more lovely sight, than a beautiful young woman upon her knees addressing her Maker in fervent prayer," and if I might presume to add my sentiments, I would say, that it is a sight at which men and angels should rejoice.

Every young and innocent woman must necessarily feel a painful diffidence on her first entrance into the bustle of life. A thorough sense of religion alone can dispel her apprehensions, give calmness to her mind, and steadiness to her conduct. For while we consider ourselves under the immediate guidance and protection of an all-wise and all-powerful Being, what have we to fear? True confidence arises from such a dependence, and fills the mind with "that sweet peace which goodness bosoms ever."

Mr Addison very justly observes, "That a mind which has the least turn to religion, naturally flies to it in affliction." We then begin to feel our own insufficiency, we are humbled by sorrow, and perhaps only then deduce real satisfaction from a thorough conviction that there is a superior Being, whose aid is graciously promised to those who sincerely seek it.

But though

"Religion's force divine is best display'd
In a desertion of all human aid,"

we must by no means presume to hope for the consolation it can bestow in the days of affliction, if we have neglected to receive and submit to its legislative authority in the hours of youth and prosperity. "You must first apply to it as the guide of life, before you can have recourse to it as the refuge of sorrow." But if laboring under the severest ills which this world can inflict, we can truly say, I have endeavoured to do my duty in the state I have been called to, I have walked humbly with my God, have made my peace with him, and patiently submit to his all-wise decrees; "such reflections will chear the lonely house of virtuous poverty, soothe the complaints of grief, lighten the pressure of old age, and furnish to the bed of sickness a cordial of more grateful relish and more sovereign virtue, than any which this world can afford."[Dr Blair's Sermons]

Though the motives which I have hitherto urged for an early attachment to our religious duties seem only to relate to the happy individual who, like Solomon, "has sought Wisdom early, and found her," there can be no doubt of the innumerable benefits which society must reap, as far as her influence extends, from the conduct and example of a truly religious woman. In whatever point of view she may be placed, as Daughter, Wife, Mother, Sister or Friend, the governing principle of her life, the love of God, will operate upon her conduct in the relative duties of her station, and render that perfect in each and every degree.

I cannot conclude this important subject, without presenting to my fair Readers that elegant portrait, which the wisest of men and divinest of poets has given them, of one whom they should endeavour to imitate, if they desire to attain happiness and honour in this life, and everlasting felicity in that to come.

"Who can find a virtuous woman? For her price is far above rubies.

The heart of her husband doth safely trust in her, so that he shall have no need of spoil.

She layeth her hands to the spindle, and her hands hold the distaff.

She stretcheth out her hand to the poor, yea, she stretcheth forth her hands to the needy.

Strength and honour are her clothing, and she shall rejoice in time to come.

She openeth her mouth with wisdom and in her tongue is the law of kindness.

She looketh well to the ways of her household, and eateth not the bread of idleness.

Her children rise up and call her blessed, her husband also, and he praiseth her.

Many daughters have done virtuously, but thou excellest them all.

Favour is deceitful, and beauty is vain, but the woman that feareth the Lord she shall be praised."

Proverbs chap. Xxxi

CONJUGAL AFFECTION

"Hail Wedded Love, mysterious law, true source
Of human offspring, sole propriety
In Paradise of all things common else;
By thee adulterous Lust was driven from men,
Among the bestial herds to range; by thee
Founded in reason, loyal, just, and pure,
Relations dear, and all the charities
Of Father, Son, and Brother, first were known."

As the union of hearts is universally allowed to be the bond of marriage, so the entering into such a connection without possessing the essence or first principle on which it should be founded, must render the ceremony of none effect, and can in reason and equity only be considered as a state of legal prostitution. To speak of conjugal felicity to the wretched victims of parental authority, of avarice, or poverty, would be absurd or cruel, as they must either be incapable of forming an idea of it, or doomed for ever to lament its loss.

I therefore, in this section, particularly address myself to the happy few whom Love unites in Hymen's rosy bands, and profess to teach the art of making their happiness as permanent as the instability of mere mortal natures will admit of.

Love is a term so very vague and indiscriminate, as it is generally applied, that it would be extremely difficult to investigate its nature from its effects, in any other case but that of marriage; as the modes, perhaps, of feeling, or at least of expressing it, vary, according to the temper, manner, or situation, of each individual who either feels or feigns the passion.

But Conjugal Affection is by no means subject to such equivocal appearances; it is tenderness heightened by passion, and strengthened by esteem. It is unmixed with any selfish or sensual allay, tending solely to promote the happiness of its object here and hereafter.

Such an elevated state of happiness as must result from the affection I have described, when mutual, must surely be the acme of human felicity. But, as the point of perfection is that of declension also, it will require much pains, but they are pleasing ones, to make the ever-turning wheel of sublunary bliss keep steady to the summit it has reached, or at least to prevent its rolling down the rugged precipice where jealousy, disgust, and grief, have marked the horrid road.

The disappointments of human life must ever be proportioned to the extravagance of our expectations. Too great an ardour to be blessed is frequently the source of misery. A life of transport is not the lot of mortals. While we accept, we should chastise our joys, "lest while we clasp we kill them."

That concord of souls which constitutes the happiness of marriage, like a full concert, requires all the parts obliged to fill their several stations in perfect time and place; for though the heart may lead the band, and set out in perfect harmony, one jarring note destroys the rapturous strain, and turns the whole to discord. For this reason, I consider a parity of understanding and temper to be as necessary towards forming an happy marriage, as an equality of years, rank and fortune.

But grant these circumstances all conjoin and make the union perfect, remember, my fair Friends, satiety succeeds to rapture, as sure as night to day. Be it your province, then, to keep your husband's heart from sinking into the incurable disease of tasteless apathy. Do not rely too much upon your personal charms, however great, to preserve the conquest they may have gained.

By a proper attention to your husband, you will easily discover the bent of his genius and inclinations. To that turn all your thoughts, and let your words and actions solely tend to that great point. The kindness of your attention will awaken his, and gratitude will strengthen his affection, imperceptibly even to himself.

Our first Parent justifies his fondness for Eve, to Raphael, upon this principle:

"Neither her outside formed so fair, & c.
So much delights me, as those graceful acts,
Those thousand decencies, that daily flow
From all her words and actions mixed with love,
And sweet compliance, which declare unfeigned
Union of mind, or in us both one soul;
Harmony to behold in wedded pair,
More grateful than harmonious sound to the ear."

In an age like this, when we may suppose that every young Lady deserves the epithet with which Adam addresses his wife, "Accomplished Eve," it must be less difficult than it might have been for their female ancestors, to secure the affections of a husband already prepossessed in their favour. Let them but exert the same talents, with the same desire of pleasing, which they shewed before marriage, and I venture to pronounce that they will succeed.

A love of power and authority is natural to men; and wherever this inclination is most indulged, will be the situation of their choice. Every man ought to be the principal object of attention in his family; of course he should feel himself happier at home than in any other place. It is, doubtless, the great business of a woman's life to render his home pleasing to her husband; he will then delight in her society, and not seek abroad for alien amusements. A husband may, possibly, in his daily excursions, see many women whom he thinks handsomer than his wife; but it is generally her fault if he meets with one that he thinks more amiable. A desire of pleasing very rarely fails of its effect; but in a wife, that desire must be managed with the nicest delicacy; it should appear rather in the result, than in the design; "not obvious, not obtrusive." These petits soins are the best supplement to our great duties, and render the commerce of life delightful. Like an elegant dessert, they complete the feast, and leave not a wish unsatisfied.

We have hitherto looked only on the pleasing side of the tapestry, and seen Marriage in its most favourable light. Let us now turn the canvas, and take a view of its defects.

Let us suppose, then, what I think the worst of all situations, an amiable young woman possessing the tenderest affection for her husband, while he, from the natural depravity and inconstancy of his nature, has withdrawn his love from her, and perhaps bestowed it on some unworthy object, to whom he devotes his time and fortune.

In such a state of wretchedness what line shall our neglected wife pursue? The first step that I would recommend to her, is, that of entering into a serious, strict, and impartial review of her own conduct, even to the minutiae of her dress, and the expressions of her looks, from the first of her acquaintance with her husband. If, after such examination, she cannot discover any faults in her manners that might have given offence, or created disgust, let her steadily pursue the same behaviour she has hitherto practised; for, if that be totally free from error, it is impossible that any alteration can give an additional efficacy to it. For to resent, or to retaliate, neither her duty, nor her religion will permit.

"To carry smiles upon the face, when discontent sits brooding at the heart," is, I confess, one of the most difficult tasks that can possibly be imposed on an ingenuous and feeling soul. But a thorough conviction that it is her province to endeavour to recal the wanderer back, for his own happiness, as well as her's, and a certainty that there are no other means of accomplishing so desirable an end, will enable her to pursue this arduous undertaking, till either her heart shall rejoice in its success, or from reiterated disappointments become indifferent to the worthless object of its former esteem and attention.

Granting the last to be the case, she has the right to expect the good opinion of the world will attend her conduct: but an higher and more certain reward awaits it; self-approbation, arising from a consciousness of having fulfilled her duty, and an assurance of having essayed the only method that was likely to insure success: for never yet was love recalled by lamentations or upbraidings. The first may sometimes, perhaps, create pity, but oftener begets contempt; and the latter never did, nor can produce any passion but instant rage, or cool determined hate.

Recollections may furnish to my fair Readers many instances where patient sufferings have been rewarded with returning love; but I think there is scarcely one to be met with, where female violence has ever conquered male outrage; or where dissipation and coquetry, though they may have alarmed the pride, ever reclaimed the alienated affections of a husband.

True love, like true virtue, shrinks not on the first attack; it will bear many shocks before it be entirely vanquished. As it contends not for victory, but for the prize, it will not display itself in the vain arts of elocution, but in the more powerful eloquence of action; it will leave nothing undone that can prove its sincerity, but it will not boast, even to its object, of what it has done; much less will it vaunt its merits to any other confidant, or complain to the world of the unkind return it has met with.

There are such a variety of circumstances which may disturb the happiness of the marriage-state, that it is impossible to specify them all; but as a virtuous woman will consider the loss of her husband's affection as the greatest calamity that can befall her, her duty and prudence will, before the evil happens, upon every occasion supply rules of conduct to herself; and the reliance she will necessarily have upon the tenderness of his attachment to her, joined to the sincerity of her's to him, will support her through every difficulty which accident, misfortune, or even imprudence, may have brought upon them. She will say, with Prior's Emma,

"Thy rise of fortune did I only wed,
From its decline determined to recede;
Did I but purpose to embark with thee,
On the smooth surface of a summer's sea,
While gentle zephyrs play in prosperous gales,
And Fortune's favour fills the swelling sails,
But would forsake the bark and make the shore,
When the winds whistle, and the tempests roar?
No, Henry, No! one sacred oath has tyed
Our loves, one destiny our lives shall guide,
Nor wild, nor deep, our common way divide."

This is the natural language of conjugal affection, this the fulfilling of the marriage vow, where self is lost in a still dearer object, where tenderness is heightened by distress, and attachment cemented even by the tears of sorrow. Such an union of souls may brave the power of Time; and I trust, that Death itself shall not be able to destroy it.

TEMPER

It has been already remarked that a parity of temper is one of the principal requisites in matrimonial happiness; and yet it is possible that too great a similarity of disposition may, in some cases, render both parties wretched. For instance, if two persons of a gay and careless turn of mind should happen to be united, both will think themselves entitled to pursue their joint or separate amusements, without being encumbered with any attention to domestic oeconomy, till even the necessary means for their support may be irretrievably lavished away.

Again, should two persons of a saturnine complexion be joined in the indissoluble bond of marriage, the natural gloominess of their dispositions will be increased by each other's converse; melancholy will become habitual, and care be heightened to despondency.

"Not minds of melancholy strain,
Still silent, or that still complain.
Can the dear bondage bless;
As well may heavenly concerts spring
From two old lutes with ne'er a string
Or none besides the bass.
Nor can the soft enchantment hold
Two jarring souls of angry mold,
The rugged and the keen;

He stopped in his earnestness to look the question, and the expression of his eyes overpowered her. "My dearest Emma," said he, "for dearest you will always be, whatever the event of this hour's conversation, my dearest, most beloved Emma – tell me at once. Say, "No" if it is to be said." She could really say nothing. "You are silent," he cried, with great animation,"absolutely silent! at present I ask no more."

Sampson's young foxes might as well
In bands of chearful wedlock dwell,
With firebrands tied between."

From these examples it is obvious, that a similitude of dispositions alone, though a strong incentive to affection, will not always ensure matrimonial felicity. And yet I am perfectly convinced, that wherever there is any material difference of sentiments or manners, there never was, or will be, a happy marriage. We naturally admire those we love, and as naturally imitate what we admire. The familiarity that arises from conformity, and a desire to please, has a superior charm to that which is merely complexional. To adopt the sentiments of a person is the most delicate proof of approbation and esteem; and perhaps the compliment is valued by our self-love, in proportion to the sacrifice which has been made of an opposite way of thinking.

That conformity of manners, as far as religion and reason will permit, is one of the indispensible duties of a Wife, will not, I believe, be denied by any one. But there are Ladies who have an art of letting their condescension appear too strongly in the act, as if submitting to the impositions of a tyrant, rather than chearfully fulfilling the obligation they had entered into at the altar – to love, honour, and obey.

The same words or actions, expressed or performed in a gracious or ungracious manner, may produce effects as differing as Love and Hate. I would, therefore, recommend it to the candidates for happiness in the marriage-state, to sacrifice to the Graces, in their conjugal demeanour, as sincerely as they do at their toilets; for good-breeding is as necessary to the preservation of domestic harmony, as it can possibly be to the general intercourse and commerce of life.

Solomon, in his description of a virtuous woman, before quoted, has furnished us with the finest idea that ever was given, of a wife's address to her husband. "She openeth her mouth with wisdom, and in her tongue is the law of kindness." And surely there exists not a being, under the form of man, who could reject such an address with scorn or insolence.

We should, however, take particular care to time our conversation with our husbands, and neither idly obtrude upon their serious hours of business or retirement, nor hastily mistake that reserve or gloom which may arise from difficulties in their affairs, abroad, for ill-temper or disgust at home.

It is the duty of a wife not only to regulate her own Temper towards her husband, but also to pay such an attention to his, as may prevent it, from ever appearing in a disagreeable light. By studiously observing the proper seasons for the different subjects on which she may have occasion to address him, she may, imperceptibly to him, and almost to herself, obtain the power of guiding his concurrence or denial.

A sensible and virtuous woman, pursuing such a line of conduct for the mutual advantage of her husband and family, without any selfish views, which only little minds are capable of, comes nearest to the idea that mortals are taught to conceive of a Guardian Angel, who, unseen, directs our doubtful choice to what is best, and leads our erring steps into the paths of happiness and peace.

I have hitherto considered this great article of Temper, only in one point of view, merely as it relates to the colloquial intercourse between a wedded pair. I come now to shew that its influence is universally extensive; and that it is one of the main springs which guides or deranges the human machine, through every station and situation of life.

An unmarried woman is very rarely said to be ill-tempered, and yet there are such prodigies in nature as young vixens, who, however they may conceal their ill-humour from their lovers and general acquaintance, will surely betray it to their parents, inmates, and servants. "A little lump leaveneth the whole," and a peevish maiden will infallibly make a cross wife; for, when once a sourness of disposition becomes habitual, there is no alkaline in nature sufficiently powerful to correct the heart-burnings and bitterness of a dissatisfied Temper. A person so affected, like one infected with the plague, necessarily spreads the contagion of discontent around her. Her parents lament the badness of her disposition; her other relations and connections are sensible of aversion, instead of affection, towards her; and her servants regret that the irksomeness of servitude is aggravated by receiving their subsistence from a tyrant, whom they can neither please, respect, or love.

As gravity, which is sometimes but another name for dullness, has been frequently mistaken for wisdom, so is chearfulness often accepted for good-humour. But that species of chearfulness which we meet with in society, that laughs in the eye, and lights up the countenance, generally proceeds rather from an ebullition of the spirits, than a designed and consistent exertion of our powers to please, and is more frequently the result of a lively than a placid disposition. As it flows from an accidental cause, its effects must necessarily be precarious; it is, therefore, subject to causeless and sudden dejection, to which habitual good-humour is by no means liable.

Distinct as these two qualities are, they have yet one property common to both, and at the same time different from what can be imputed to any other happy endowment, which is, that they are most meritorious where they are least natural. An idiot may be constitutionally good-humoured, and a villain be chearful, from a glow of health or a flow of spirits; but that species of good-humour which is the result of sense, virtue, and gratitude to Providence, will be uniform in its appearance, and consistent in its manners; it will not, like an April day, lour [lower] and shine almost in the same moment; nor, like the flaming heats of July, will the brightness of the meridian sun foretel the approaching thunder; but clear, calm, and undisturbed, shall it shine on even to its latest hour.

Such a blessed state of mind must necessarily communicate the happiness it feels to all around it. "Like the smooth stream, it reflects every object in its just proportion, and in its fairest colours; while the turbulent and ruffled spirit, like troubled waters, renders back the images of things distorted and broken, and communicates to them all that disordered motion which arises solely from its own agitation." [Dr Blair]

This beautiful simile has a double claim to female attention; for rage, jealousy, or any other ungentle passion, deform the fairest face almost as much as they degrade the mind, and "can unsex the loveliest of the lovely kind, e'en from the top to the toe."

But there is a higher and a stronger motive than any I have yet mentioned for "possessing our souls in gentleness," if we presume to call ourselves Christians. Shall the disciple of a suffering Saviour dare to resent with furious outrage the real or imaginary injuries she may receive? Or can she kneel before the throne of Mercy, and supplicate the God of Peace and Good-will to Man, for pardon or protection, while her heart is agitated with a spirit of malice or revenge towards a fellow-creature frail as her wretched self? This were an insult upon piety, a mockery of devotion!

We are assured that God rejects the proud, and that an humble and a contrite heart are precious in his sight.

Shall we than cast away the heart-felt transport of thinking ourselves under the guidance and protection of an Almighty Providence, to sacrifice to Moloch? and give away the birthright of the redeemed, for the sad privilege of torturing ourselves? For Providence has wisely ordained, that all the malevolent passions of the human breast should prey upon their possessors. Peace never dwelt with envy, rage, or hate.

As marriage, among Christians, is of divine institution, all married persons should consider a proper conduct towards each other, as the fulfilling of a religious duty. To promote harmony, peace, order, and happiness, in their families, is the mutual and undoubted obligation both of man and wife. This rule once established and reduced to practice, even libertines will own that marriage is the happiest state on earth; but when the fiends of discord, rage, confusion, and misery, usurp the place of those dear Houshold Gods, their very opposite, we must agree with Dr Tillotson, and own that such a state is but "a lesser hell, in passage to the greater."

Be it your care, then, my gentle and much-interested Readers, to reverse this sad idea, and by the mildness of your manners, and the sweetness of your tempers, render the marriage-state a lesser heaven, in passage to the greater.

NEATNESS

Neatness is the offspring of Decency, and the parent of Elegance; and to her, perhaps, are my fair countrywomen more indebted for the power of making and preserving their conquests, than to any other of those numerous charms which they possess in common with the rest of their sex.

At this polished era, when elegance, at least as far as it relates to form and dress, seems to be elevated almost into a science, which is become more the object of study and attention than any of those which are to be found in the Encyclopedia, it may seem superfluous to say much upon the subject of this chapter; but though I should wish neatness and elegance to be ever united, yet I would not, by any means, have them confounded together, as they certainly are as distinct, as light and shade in painting; and like them too, when happily combined, they mutually reflect grace on each other, while the charming result of both, amounts to "something than beauty more."

In the beginning of this almost finished century, the most refined Moralist of his age [Addison] or nation told his fair contemporaries, that "wrapping-gowns and dirty linen were the bane of conjugal love." Yet in those days our grandmothers might possibly have thought they dressed as elegantly as the present race of young women imagine they do now. But then, less enlightened than their happier descendants, they might vainly presume, that the brilliancy of their charms, when heightened by dress, and animated by the gaiety of an opera or a ball, could efface the disgust which a husband might have conceived from the indelicacy of their appearance in their own apartments. How vain, indeed, must such an idea seem to us, who know that disgust is, perhaps, the only unconquerable sentiment of the human mind, and that it can never be detached from the unfortunate object which has once inspired it! The application of this knowledge is too obvious to need any comment.

The qualities of Neatness extend much farther than to the exterior, or even the interior of dress; the house as well as person, nay the mind, of an accomplished woman should be regulated by the same spirit; for it is very possible to meet with a littered head though "bien coiffée", and a slatternly mind in a very elegant form.

Neatness is to the person what purity is to the mind. In many instances they are so perfectly analogous, that they seem to be rather a simple than a complex idea. But though their qualities appear so very similar, they are, alas! at some times disunited. They have, however, one striking characteristic common to both, which is, that art will, upon examination, be always found deficient to imitate their unaffected excellence.

I shall conclude these few imperfect hints with Lord Lyttelton's beautiful lines upon the same subject:

"Do thou, my Fair, endeavour to possess
An elegance of mind as well as dress."

DOMESTIC AMUSEMENT

Variety is, in general, the very essence of amusement. How then is it possible to fix an idea which exists but in change? Or how define a term, the meaning of which may be understood so differently by different persons?

Yet still every human mind requires relaxation, and amusement will be sought, and should be found, by persons of every condition in life. Those whom Providence has place in elevated situations of rank or fortune, have undoubtedly an infinite advantage over their inferiors, in this article, as a proper and liberal education must have afforded them an early taste for two of the most elegant amusements that can be enjoyed, namely, Reading and Music. Whoever has felt the charms of these delightful avocations, will never be subject to that miserable complaint called Ennui, nor lament the want of company or employment for a few hours in any part of a short day, for such the longest will seem to those who can so well employ it.

Drawing and Painting are also delightful resources to those whom favouring Genius has led to such sweet arts; but talents for these are rare, and those who are so peculiarly gifted, should be particularly grateful for such rare endowments.

But besides these inexhaustible funds of rational amusement, there are still an infinite number of minor resources, which may afford us occupations sufficient to combat the tediousness of life, even supposing it to be passed in solitude. The great variety of needleworks, which the ingenious women of other countries, as well as of our own, have invented, will furnish us with constant and amusing employment; and though our labours of the loom may not equal a Minerva's or an Aylesbury's, yet if they unbend the mind by fixing its attention on the progress of any elegant or imitative art, they answer the purpose of domestic amusement; and when the higher duties of our situation do not call forth our exertion, we may feel the satisfaction of knowing that we are, at least, innocently employed.

While under the influence of this calm sentiment, we shall be less apt to rush into the torrent of dissipation, where conjugal happiness is too frequently lost, or, at least, endangered, by the poisonous gales of flattery, which, though breathed from coxcombs whom we may in our hearts despise, will in some sort render us despicable; for no woman listens to adulation whose vanity is not flattered by it.

But there is still another danger, from which constant and innocent amusement may help to preserve us; I mean the destructive vortex of a Gaming-table, where every soft and feminine grace is swallowed up by Avarice; where our internal peace must necessarily be destroyed by the anxious solicitude of hope and fear, which can only terminate in the most painful of all feelings to an ingenuous mind, the consciousness of having voluntarily erred.

As the world is at present constituted, it is almost impossible for any person who mixes with it to avoid play; and cards, as a mere amusement, may sometimes be deemed an innocent one. Conversation is not to be met with in large and mixed companies; and a card-table, considered as an universal leveller, may have its use, by placing the weak and timid on a par with the most lively and overbearing. But in order to render play what it should be, an amusement merely, a line must be drawn by the circumstances of each individual, with regard to the expence for

"What's in the Captain but a choleric word,
Is in the Soldier downright blasphemy."

There can be, therefore, but one general rule devised, which is, never to play for more than you can afford to lose, without breaking in upon the necessary claims of your family, your dress or your charities. I shall only add, that those who engage in play on any other terms than what I have mentioned, will soon discover that they have exchanged their down for thorns; and will, perhaps, too late remember the just picture which Mr Pope has drawn of those unhappy female beings who pass, not spend, a life of idleness and dissipation.

"Mark how the world its veterans rewards,
A youth of frolic, an old age of cards;
Fair to no purpose, artful to no end,
Young without lovers, old without a friend,"

FRIENDSHIP

The Antients ranked friendship in the second class of human virtues; and many are the instances recorded in history, where its energy has produced effects almost divine. Considered in its perfect strength and beauty, it certainly is the most sublime, because the least selfish, affection of the soul.

Honour is its very essence; courage, frankness, and generosity, its unalienable properties. Such is the idea delivered down to us of this noble sentiment, by its contemporary writers, "who together flourished, and together fell:" for some centuries have elapsed, since this exalted phenomenon has deigned to appear among the degenerate Sons of Men; and, like a mutilated statue, it is now become rather an object of admiration to a few virtuosi in philosophy, than a subject for general emulation.

Montaigne, amongst the Moderns, seems to have felt a stronger emanation of this virtue, than any Author I am acquainted with; and tho' the utmost stretch of his warm imagination gives us but a faint ray of its ancient lustre, yet even this slight resemblance appears too strong for our weak eyes, and seems rather to dazzle than attract our regards.

Our contemporary, Dr Young, has left us several very beautiful descriptions of Friendship, which, though deficient of that fire which not only blazed but burned in this ancient virtue, are, however, sufficient to form both our theory and our practice upon.

"True Friendship warms, it raises, it transports,
Like music pure the joy, without allay,
Whose very rapture is tranquillity."

This is a very pleasing and just description of Friendship in the abstract; but it wants that energy which particular attachments add to all our sentiments, and without which, like a winter's sun, they shine, but do not warm.

The same Author has given us a more interesting, tho', perhaps, less elevated idea of this affection of the mind, in his address to a particular person:

"Lorenzo, pride suppress, nor hope to find
A friend, but what has found a Friend in thee."

This is a new, and I think a just, light in which we may consider this sentiment: for though love may be formed without sympathy, Friendship never can. It is, even in its degenerate state, an affection that cannot subsist in vicious minds; and among the most virtuous, it requires a parity of sentiment, manners, and rank, for its basis. Of all the nice ties and dependencies which constitute the happiness or misery of life, it is the most delicate, and even the most fragile. Wealth cannot purchase, nor gifts ensure, its permanence. "The chirping of birds in cages bears as much resemblance to the vocal music of the woods, as bought courtesies to real friendship." The Great, alas! rarely enjoy this blessing; vanity and emulation prevent its growth among equals; and the humiliating condescension with which superiors sometimes deign to affect Friendship for their inferiors, strikes at the very foundation of the sentiment; from which there can only arise a tottering superstructure, whose pillars, like those of modern composition, bear the gloss, but want the durable quality of the mental marble, sincerity. Yet there have been instances, though rare, of real Friendship between persons of different ranks in life, particularly Henry the Fourth and Sully; but the virtues of the latter placed him on a level with Monarchs, and the magnanimity of the former made him sensible of their equality.

Yet how often are complaints uttered by disappointed pride, against the ingratitude of those whom they have honoured with the title of Friend, nay, and have even served and obliged as such; without reflecting that obligations to a generous mind are insults, when accompanied with the least slight or mortification.

On the other hand we, perhaps, too willingly attach ourselves to our superiors. Our self-love is flattered by their approbation, and it naturally imagines it can only be for our good and amiable qualities that they like or distinguish us. But tho'"love, like death, makes all distinction void,"Friendship has no such levelling power. Superiority of rank or fortune is generally felt by the person who possesses either; and they are entitled to some degree of praise, if they do not make others feel it also.

Let those, then, who have delicate minds, remember that equality is the true basis of Friendship; let them set a just value on their own worth, as well as on the inebriating smiles of greatness, and not expose their sensibility to the pangs it must sustain, on discovering that neither virtues or talents can always keep the scale of Friendship steady, when opposed to the adventitious circumstances of high birth, or great fortune.

Thus far my remarks upon this subject are general. Let me now apply them to their use for whom this little work is peculiarly designed, by earnestly recommending it to every young married woman to seek the friend of her heart in the husband of her affection. There, and there only, is that true equality, both of rank and fortune, strengthened by mutual interest and cemented by mutual pledges, to be found. There only condescensions will not mortify, as they will be concessions but of kindness, not of pride. There, and there only, will she be sure to meet with reciprocal confidence, unfeigned attachment, and tender solicitude, to soothe her every care. The ties of wedded love will be rivetted by the bands of Friendship; the virtues of her mind, when called forth by occasion, will unfold themselves by degrees to her husband's perception, like the opening rose before the morning ray; and when its blooming colour fades upon her cheek, its sweetness shall remain within the very foldings of his heart, from recollection of her sense and worth. Happy are the pairs so joined; yea, blessed are they who are thus doubly united!

As the word Friendship is at present generally understood to be a term of little import, or at most that extends merely to a preference of liking, or esteem; I would by no means exclude my fair Readers from that kind of commerce which is now accepted under that title, in society. But even this sort of connection requires much caution in the choice of its object; for I should wish it might be restrained to one; and that one ought to obtain this preference, from the qualities of the heart rather than those of the head. A long and intimate acquaintance can alone discover the former; the latter are easily and willingly displayed; for love without esteem is as a shower, soon spent. The heart is the spring of affections, but the mind is their reservoir.

For this reason, it always appears to me a proof of mutual merit, when two sisters, or two young women, who have been brought up together, are strongly attached to each other; and I will admit, that while they remain unmarried, such a connection is capable of forming a pure and disinterested friendship, provided that the sympathy of their affections does not tend to make them like or admire the same male object; for though Love may, Friendship cannot exist with jealousy.

"Reserve will wound it, and distrust destroy."

That great master of the human heart Shakespeare has shewn us, that maidenly attachment is no match for the stronger passion of love.

"Is all the counsel that we two have shared,
The sister vows, the hours that we have spent,
When we have chid the hasty-footed time
For parting us – O! and is all forgot?
All school-days, friendship, childhood innocence.
We, Hermia, like two artificial Gods,
Created with our needles both one flower,
Both on one sampler, sitting on one cushion,
Both warbling of one song, both in one key:
As if our hands, our sides, voices, and minds
Had been incorp'rate."
(Midsummer Night's Dream)

If such an almost instinctive affection as that between Hermia and Helena was so quickly dissolved by the intruder Love, I fear there are but few female friendships that will better stand the test. And to a delicate mind it may appear a breach, perhaps, of those "sister vows," when one of the parties enters into another and more forcible engagement; for Love is an imperious and engrossing tyrant; of course the gentler affection must give way and retire within itself, as the sensitive plant shrinks back, oppressed by too intense an heat.

In my small experience, I have never seen the same degree of attachment subsist between two ladies after marriage as before, excepting they were sisters. The bands of natural affection are not loosened by new engagements; but those of choice or casualty necessarily become relaxed by the addition of a new object, as extension lessens strength.

The minds of most young women seem, and indeed ought to do so in reality, to acquire a new bent after marriage: scenes different from those to which they had been accustomed, open to their view; different objects engross their attention;

every state has its cares; and, from the queen to the peasant, every wife has duties to fulfil. Frivolous amusements are, or should be, renounced, for the more pleasing and respectable avocations of an affectionate Wife, a tender Mother, and a beloved and honoured Matron of a family.

I hope it is impossible that I should be so far misunderstood, as to be thought to exclude married women from any innocent pleasure or rational amusement that is suited to their age, rank, or fortune. I would not only ensure but augment their happiness, and shall therefore say with Othello.

"Where virtue is, these are most virtuous."

But still there is, or should be, a difference in the enjoyment of their pleasures; between the thoughtless gaiety of girls, and the decent chearfulness of married women. The first is bright and transient, as the youthful glow of health and vivacity that blooms upon the cheek; the latter should express that tranquil joy which flows from true content.

I may be thought to have somewhat wandered from the particular subject of this chapter, though, I hope, not from the general object of the work. I shall now conclude with observing, that as the characters and conduct of even her common acquaintance reflect honour or disgrace upon a young married woman, she will be an inevitable sharer in that degree of respect or contempt which her chosen friend possesses in the esteem of the world: and though its censures may sometimes involve the innocent with the guilty; yet, in general, there is no fairer way of forming our opinions of persons we do not know, than from their intimate associates.

There is something still more alarming to be dreaded for a young woman who is thoughtless enough to form indiscriminate friendships. There is a lightness of mind and manners in many women, who, though free from actual vice, have lost that delicate sensibility which Heaven has placed in female minds as the out-guard of modesty. The rosy blush that gives the intuitive alarm to decency, even before the perceptions of the mind are awake to danger, glows not upon their cheek; the snowy purity of innocence beams not upon their dauntless forehead, though it may still retain its whiteness. Their minds may be course, however delicate their form; and their manners unfeminine, even without being masculine.

An intimacy with such persons is, of all others, the most dangerous. The frankness and liveliness of their conversation render them too generally agreeable, and they frequently undermine the principles of virtue, before we find it necessary to stand upon our guard.

As the Platonic system has been long exploded, it is almost unnecessary to warn my fair Readers against particular intimacies with the other sex, when not closely connected with them by the ties of blood or affinity. The whole system of Nature must change, and the tyger and the lamb live peaceably together, before a sincere and disinterested friendship can subsist between an amiable young woman and a man not nearly related to her, who has not passed his grand climacteric. A man of such an age, possessed of sense and virtue, may perhaps be a kind and useful Mentor; but if a married woman is happy enough to meet with a proper and affectionate return from the first object I have recommended to her choice, she cannot stand in need of any other Friend.

PARENTAL AND FILIAL AFFECTION

Parental Affection seems to be so perfectly instinctive, that when any unhappy object appears to be deficient in this

"I do not care. Mr Thorpe had no business to invent any such message. If I had thought it right to put it off, I could have spoken to Miss Tilney myself. This is only doing it in a ruder way; and how do I know that Mr Thorpe has – he may be mistaken again, perhaps; he led me into one act of rudeness by his mistake on Friday. Let me go, Mr Thorpe: Isabella, do not hold me."

natural sentiment, I consider such a person as one who has been unfortunately born deaf or blind; that is, in a state of deprivation of some of those faculties which Providence has been graciously pleased to render inherent in our nature, in its perfect formation.

If Milton deplored the loss of sight, as shutting knowledge at one entrance out, with how much more reason may they, who are insensible to the fond and tender sensations of parental love, lament, that the fairest page in Nature's volume, the infant mind, appears to them a blank; and transports, such as parents only feel, from their cold hearts for evermore shut out!

That every species of animals have sometimes produced monsters, is certain, but, by the goodness of Providence, they are few in number, when compared with the happy multitudes who are perfect in their several orders of existence, It is, therefore, unnecessary to pursue this painful idea further; so that I shall only add, to the honour of England, that an unfeeling parent is among us a character almost as singular as detestable.

But as affection in its natural progression rather descends than ascends, we sometimes see instances of deficiency in the returns of filial affection to parental love. Whenever this failure appears in persons of otherwise good and amiable dispositions, I am inclined to believe that there must have been something peculiarly wrong in the bias of their education, or the conduct of their parents towards them; for in a state of infancy every child must naturally love its parents; they are the first objects which awaken in us the ideas of power and kindness; of a power that enables, and a kindness that prompts, to supply all our little wants, and to soothe and alleviate all our pains and distresses. Long before we are able to develop these ideas, they naturally produce the almost instinctive sensations of reverence, gratitude, and love. These happy feelings of a virtuous mind

"Grow with our growth, and strengthen with our strength,"

till sensation becomes sentiment, which can never be totally eradicated, though it may sometimes be restrained, or even overborne for a while, by some particular species of unkindness, severity, or injustice.

But though the sentiments of filial affection are so natural to every good heart, that Sovereign Power which formed us, "and knoweth whereof we are made," has thought proper to command the exertion of this virtue in its fullest extent, by the emphatic term of "Honour thy Father and thy Mother", and has been graciously pleased to add the promise of length of days to those who fulfil this law.

When the ties of natural affection are thus enforced by the Divine sanction, it appears almost impossible that any casualty should dissolve this double band, or that it should even be weakened by any other attachment.

The union which is formed by wedded love, can never slacken or abate its strength; for in liberal minds the encrease of happiness, like the sun's beams upon a fertile soil, calls every virtue forth; the tender charities which gladden life are ripened and matured beneath its influence; while the flowers of connubial fondness bloom fairest, and are sweetest to the sense, when they grow on the rich stem of filial love: and a husband must be either weak or tyrannic, who does not rejoice in the kindness and attention of his wife to those who have been early and are nearly connected with her.

Family attachments have this advantage over all others, that they are not subject to satiety. Parental fondness is augmented by the growth and expansion of every charm and merit in a child; and as it naturally happens that the parents begin to decline when the children have arrived at their zenith, reverence for their age and gratitude for their kindness, combined with the tender apprehension of losing them, add strength to our former affectionate feelings, and awaken that almost divine enthusiasm which inspired Pope's filial prayer:

"Me let the tender office long engage.
To rock the cradle of declining Age;
Explore the thought, explain the asking eye,
And keep awhile a parent from the sky!"

The proportions of our affection and esteem must necessarily, because naturally, be limited by the respective merits of the persons on whom they are conferred. Reason admits not of superstitious attachments in point of sentiment. But no demerit in a parent can absolve a child from that duty which has the double sanction both of God and Nature. How truly are they to be pitied, who, either from their own or their parents' defects, are unhappily rendered insensible to the virtuous transport of giving joy to those who gave them being! who, incapable of the pleasing alacrity arising from filial affection, fulfil the requests or wishes of a parent with the same reluctant coldness that they would execute the commands of a severe master!

Parental authority is certainly abrogated by that of a husband – "we cannot serve two masters." But we can love a father and a husband, a mother and a son, with as pure and unmixed affection, as if our whole heart was devoted to any one of these individuals. Family connections, so far from being dissolved by marriage, are rather strengthened by the addition of a new member, and should continue to hold the first place in the society of a young married woman. If she is so happy as to approve, and be approved by, her husband's family, her love for him will incorporate them in her esteem with her own. She will naturally become the center of their mutual attachments and regard; while her amiable and endearing influence extending to each individual, shall unite them all in one complete and happy circle.

OECONOMY

This is a subject which depends so entirely upon circumstances, that, like the chameleon, it must necessarily take its hue from the surrounding objects: but though obliged to vary its appearance from its different situations, it has still some fixed and determinate principles which constitute its essence, and preserve its name in every condition of life. Oeconomy may be compared to an isthmus placed between a continent and a peninsula, between profusion and parsimony, bearing equal relation to both. It is a line drawn by the hand of Reason upon the human mind to restrain the thoughtless excess of extravagance, too often miscalled generosity, and at the same time to set bounds to the meanest of all vices, avarice.

Neither rank nor riches can place any person above oeconomy; and perhaps those who possess such advantages in the highest degree, have the greatest occasion for the practice of this humble virtue. – "Where much is given, much is required," as well in the literal as the figurative sense of the expression; and when those who are blessed with affluence consider themselves, as they are bound to do, but as stewards for the poor, they must surely reflect that dissipation and extravagance are not the use, but the abuse, of that store which has been thus entrusted to their care, and that such misapplication cannot entitle them to fair acquittance from the great Giver of all good.

But were we to confine our views even to this dim spot, we shall find that oeconomy is, in every situation of life, a requisite and necessary duty incumbent on human nature. They must be very young indeed, who have not heard

"Of numbers, once in Fortune's lap high-fed,
Who now solicit the cold hand of Charity!"

And what must then be the feelings of a generous heart, which from its indolence, or the vile indulgence of some fond caprice, has become self-deprived of that transcendant delight which Angels share with Men, of wiping off the bitter tear of woe, of soothing the afflicted heart, and bidding peace and joy revisit the sad mansions of despair!

Oeconomy is as perfectly inconsistent with avarice as with extravagance. Whenever it degenerates into penuriousness, it ceases to be a virtue, and appears even a less pardonable fault than its contrary extreme; for extravagance may be prompted by generosity, but selfishness can have no motive that is not mean. Oeconomy is founded in that justice which we owe to others, and in that proper respect which we owe to ourselves: these principles, happily united, form the true source of liberality and independence.

There is an oeconomy of time, too, as well as of fortune, which I would earnestly recommend. A little attention to this very important article would serve to lighten that sad load of which we oft complain, while yet with childish fondness we lament its flight! perhaps unknowing that it is within our power to wing its speed, or to arrest its course; or, perhaps, still worse, not reflecting that we shall be accountable for this rich, this sacred deposit, when time itself shall be no more!

For the proper oeconomy of this treasure, one general rule is sufficient for all ranks and situations- Employ your time- "Time wasted is existence, used is life," and every condition and stage of life has its necessary and peculiar employments.

Action is the great spring on which Creation turns; it is that which preserves and harmonizes all. Even things inanimate, trees, plants, and flowers, obey the voice of Nature, and act in their own sphere. Unbidden they send forth their fruits and odours, and pay their tribute to Creation's laws. The elements themselves subsist by motion. Without its actuating spirit the earth no more could turn upon its axis; the fire would be extinct, and air and water stagnate to putrefaction. Shall Man alone, the master-work of Heaven, rust in dull indolence, and, sinking in enervate sloth, debase his nature beneath the trodden clod? formed to contemplate all the works of God, to think upon the wonders of past times, and raise his future hopes to an eternity!

"Time is eternity;
Pregnant with all eternity can give,
Pregnant with all that makes Archangels smile! –
Who murders time, he crushes in the birth
A power aetherial, only not adored."

No reasoning being can doubt, but that the use or abuse of time must mark our future fate, as we ourselves ordain:

"The Spirit walks of each departed day
And smiles an Angel, or a Fury frowns."

But for a moment let us admit that conscience could be lulled to rest on beds of roses, or that the waste of time might not be deemed a vice; is there on earth a human being so lost to every sense of its own dignity as to acquiesce in bare existence, and to look back upon the sum of that existence as a blank? This last argument appears to some so fully sufficient to awaken that noble pride, that true self-estimation which Heaven has implanted in our souls, for the great purpose of exalting our nature above the subordinate classes of animals, who are debarred the glorious prerogative of looking forward with humble hope to an happy immortality, that I should think any other incitement would be superfluous upon this subject: which I shall therefore conclude with the interesting picture which the last Author quoted above has given, of those happy few who have made a right use of that treasure that Heaven has pleased to entrust them with.

"Where shall I find him? Angels, tell me where!
Your golden wings now hov'ring o'er him shed
Protection, now are waving in applause.
To that blest Son of Foresight! Lord of Fate!
That awful independent on To-morrow!
Whose work is done–who triumphs in the past;
Whose yesterdays looks backwards with a smile,
Nor, like the Parthian, wound him as they fly."

CONCLUSION

As I have now, though perhaps but faintly, touched upon the duties most essential in the marriage-state, it appears to me unnecessary to pursue this work any farther; though I am certain there are many follies, not to give them a harsher name, incident to my sex, which are not even glanced at in these Essays. The most glaring, perhaps, that has been left unnoticed, is the universal spirit of dissipation which seems to reign among all ranks of women. But though I have not particularly attacked this Arch-demon, this greatest enemy to domestic happiness, I hope I have in some degree undermined his batteries, and sapped his intrenchments in the female heart. At least, I have offered to those who chuse to accept them, the powerful auxiliaries of Religion, Conjugal Affection, and Parental Love, to oppose his force, and render them superior to his allurements; for those who serve under the banner of these mild Virtues, will never fall a prey to the tyrannic power of Vice, however it may be supported by custom, or adorned by the seductive arts of fashion.

As these Essays are meant to be generally useful, it would be impossible to confine their precepts to any particular rank or situation; of course there can be no rules laid down for the conduct of individuals under any peculiar circumstances: and indeed the whole Work may rather be considered as a sketch, from which the intelligent mind may deduce inferences and make applications, than as a regular plan to be diligently pursued.

Uncandid and unfavourable as the present times may be deemed to moral literature, and unequal as I may be thought to so arduous a subject as that I have undertaken, I still presume to hope there is no Critic so severe as to deny me the merit of meaning well, though I may have fallen infinitely short of the real motive that prompted this publication; which is, to restore my fair Countrywomen to that pre-eminence they formerly held over the rest of their sex through the known world, and to bring back that glorious aera when the Epitaph of the Lucas family, characterized the whole British Nation:

"All the Brothers were valiant,
And all the Sisters virtuous."

I have humbly presumed to lay this little Work at the feet of our most amiable and gracious Queen, whose private virtues, as a Wife and Mother, add lustre to her exalted rank, and would adorn the Throne of Universal Monarchy.

FINIS

THE TWO HUSBANDS; or, the Causes of Happiness or Discontent in the Matrimonial State.
(*The New Lady's Magazine*, February 1787)

The object of every one is Happiness; but the permanence of earthly happiness not being the lot of humanity, intirely subverts the system of those who falsely imagine it is attainable here. There are, doubtless, certain degrees of it which naturally occur as each individual can meet the frowns of fortune with a serene, unruffled temper; and what can more conduce to this than that sweetness of mind which so generously characterizes and distinguishes the female sex? For they, with every little winning art, correct the petulant and acrimonious humour which a chain of unlucky events may occasion. In the arms of an affectionate wife we find refuge in every exigence; for she, with an honest sympathy, takes part in our affliction, and equally shares both our happiness or distress; in sickness she endeavours to soothe and stifle the tortures of disease, and employs every means in her power to restore us to our former health and chearfulness. What has been said in commendation of the matrimonial state is not without exception; for too many, we fear, meet with a treatment diametrically opposite to this, the truth of which we shall beg leave to illustrate with a contrasted comparison of two persons, whom we shall call by the names of Adrastus and Philander.

Adrastus was brought up to business : Philander was born to a small estate. Adrastus, after travelling for experience and improvement, settled in a small but pleasant market-town in Yorkshire, where proving successful, and considerably improving the little he had to begin with, he paid his addresses, and was married to the amiable Miss S____, a young lady of small fortune, but possessed of all those riches of the mind that constitute the affectionate wife, the tender mother, and the disinterested friend. Adrastus himself, a deserving character, and the pattern of honesty and plain dealing, lives in complete harmony with the partner of his bed, and Heaven has blessed them with two beautiful children, the happy produce of ten years uninterrupted love. Can we doubt that an union, founded on such principles as these, can fail of happiness! Certainly no. Was an honest and disinterested affection the stimulating motive and basis on which all our marriages were founded, we should hear of very few that proved unhappy.

Philander having received an education suitable to his rank, married a lady of a very large fortune, and, being of a narrow disposition, the desire of accumulating riches probably operated with greater strength than love. But, however that be, it is certain that ever since the celebration of their nuptials (exclusive of what is called the honeymoon), they have lived in a continual jarring and discontent. – Philander, though abounding in affluence, scarcely ever sits down to table with an unclouded brow; but what else can be expected from a contrariety of disposition? Nature has bestowed on his lady a gay, lively turn, which not coinciding with Philander's scheme of mean, narrow, oeconomy, is the fatal cause of dissatisfaction and uneasiness. How different to this is the life of Adrastus? The stinting hand of frugality furnishes his table with decency and sufficiency, and withal that invaluable dish, which Philander is not able to purchase; – we mean content. A look of satisfaction is reciprocally exchanged between him and his wife, whilst the dear pledges of their love, like two olive branches, (the emblems of peace), grace their table with innocence, and crown their repast with thankfulness. Thus lives Adrastus, devoting every leisure hour his avocation allows, to the company of his wife and children: a state of earthly felicity that no one is able to describe but those that experience it. And now, ye fair, give us leave to address ourselves to you.

Let not the transient blaze of false alluring hopes eclipse your understandings, nor suffer yourselves to be carried away by the torrent of splendor, or misled by the gilding of equipage; for these, to the gay and unthinking part, have a thousand charms and incitements, but, too often, under all this penciled grandeur and magnificence, conceal the barbed arrow of discontent, which inflicts an incurable wound. Study not to aggrandize yourselves and family at the expence of happiness, for happiness in a moss-grown cot is preferable to all the honours transferred in the drawing-room without it. Let the man, on whom you place your affection, be prudent, sensible, and discerning; but chiefly (before you are united to him) lay aside all interested views, and weigh in the scales of reason, the love you bear him; judge if his be equivalent to yours: if so, you need not doubt but it will answer your utmost expectation, and, when united, you will live with real satisfaction, and answer aright the end of matrimony.

ON NUPTIAL HAPPINESS.
(*The New Lady's Magazine or Companion for the Fair Sex*, June 1788)

> Be but a little deaf and blind,
> And happiness you'll surely find.

The causes of happiness in the married state are various, and arise from different quarters; the tempers, dispositions, circumstances, and conditions of both parties, whether husband or wife, may, and often do, prove the sources of discord and infelicity to the end of life; trifles are frequently the occasion of uneasiness, and too often of a lasting discontent; a word, yea, sometimes I have known a look, has, by being misconstrued, been the cause of serious disputes between the married pair, and such disputes as have terminated in a settled coolness and indifference, therefore every couple should be very cautious of letting trifles break in upon their domestic peace and comfort.

Whenever a lady finds her husband inclinable to dispute about insignificant matters, or ready to be offended at mere trifles, let her study and endeavour to act prudently and wisely, and make proper allowances for his particular temper and unhappy disposition; for want of this, many a wife is rendered miserable; her life a burden to her, and her situation much to be pitied. – Would every married couple, whether rich or poor, daily attend to, and practice what the motto to this essay recommends, they would find themselves well rewarded for their pains, however difficult they might experience the attempt. It must be acknowledged, no little self-denial, command of temper, and resolution, are necessary upon many occasions to practice this general rule for the promotion of matrimonial happiness but that it is attainable, and well worth the trial, no one can deny. Therefore let me earnestly beg the fair sex to resolve without delay to make the trial and doubt not of all desirable success attending it.

G.W.

N.B. Husbands, as well as wives, will do well to take the above advice, if they wish to be happy, as both sexes have their feelings, and too often discover them.

A Pair of Matrimonial Portraits
(*The Lady's Monthly Museum*, March 1799)
The Good Wife

The good wife is one who, ever mindful of the solemn contract which she hath entered into, is strictly and conscientiously virtuous, constant and faithful to her husband; chaste, pure and unblemished in every thought, word and deed. She is humble and modest from reason and conviction, submissive from choice and obedient from inclination: what she acquires by love and tenderness, she preserves by prudence and discretion; she makes it her business to serve, and her pleasure to oblige her husband; as conscious that every thing which promotes his happiness must in the end contribute to her own; her tenderness relieves his cares, her affection softens his distress, her good humour and complacency lessen and subdue his affliction. Lastly, as a Christian, she looketh up with an eye of gratitude to the great Dispenser and Disposer of all things, to the husband of the widow, and father of the fatherless, intreating his divine favour and assistance in this and every other moral and religious duty.

The Good Husband

The good husband is one who, wedded not by interest but by choice, is constant, as well from inclination as from principle;

She had only time, however, to move closer to the table where
he had been writing, when footsteps were heard returning; the
door opened; it was himself. He begged their pardon, but he had
forgotten his gloves, and instantly crossing the room to the writing
table, and standing with his back towards Mrs Musgrove, he drew
out a letter from under the scattered paper, placed it before Anne
with eyes of glowing entreaty fixed on her for a moment, and hastily
collecting his gloves, was again out of the room, almost before
Mrs Musgrove was aware of his being in it – the work of an instant.

he treats his wife with delicacy as a woman, with tenderness as a friend; he attributes her follies to weakness, her imprudence to her inadvertency; he passes them over, therefore, with good nature, and pardons them with indulgence: all his care and industry are employed for her welfare; all his strength and power are exerted for her support and protection: he is more anxious to preserve his own character and reputation, because her's is blended with it. Lastly, the good husband is pious and religious, that he may animate her faith by his practice, and enforce the precepts of Christianity by his own example; that, as they join to promote each other's happiness in this world, they may unite to insure eternal joy and felicity in that which is to come.

THE WAY TO KEEP HIM
(*The Family Magazine: or Repository of Religious Instruction and Rational Amusement*, October 1788)

Ye Fair, possest of ev'ry charm,
To captivate the will,
Whose smiles can rage itself disarm,
Whose frowns at once can kill.

Say, will you deign the verse to hear,
Where flatt'ry bears no part
An honest verse that flows sincere
And candid from the heart.

Great is your pow'r, but greater yet,
Mankind it might engage,
If, as ye all can make a net,
Ye all could make a cage.

Each nymph, a thousand hearts may take,
For who's to beauty blind?
But to what end a pris'ner make,
Unless you've strength to bind?

Attend the counsel often told,
Too often told in vain;
Learn that best art, the art to hold,
And lock the lover's chain.

Gamesters to little purpose win,
And lose again as fast,
Though beauty may the chain begin
T'is sweetness makes it last.

A Country Bride and Bridegroom. From a painting by Francis Wheatley.

Notes on Primary Sources

The New Lover's Instructor; or, Whole Art of Courtship. Being the Lover's Complete Library and Guide; and containing full and complete Instructions concerning Love, Courtship, and Marriage.

This manual, containing contributions from a number of people, was compiled by Charles Freeman and Charlotte Dorrington. It was published around 1780. Intended as a template for readers to use during courtship, *The New Lover's Instructor* contains love letters in prose and verse, cards of compliment and wedding invitations. An advertisement in the Norfolk *Chronicle* of 22 April 1780 recommended that this book should 'be perused by every young Man and Woman in the Kingdom.'

The Whole Duty of a Woman: or, a Guide to the Female Sex. From the age of Sixteen to Sixty, &c. Being Directions, How Women of all Qualities and Conditions, ought to Behave themselves in the various Circumstances of this Life, for them obtaining not only Present, but Future Happiness.

This manual, which was written in 1761, provides advice to virgins, married women and widows covering such topics as female accomplishments, bringing up children, managing servants and household economy. It also contains a number of recipes, and instructions for cures for a variety of ailments and maladies, to help women in their duties as housekeepers and carers.

The identity of the author of this manual is not known, but it is thought that, despite being written from a female viewpoint, it may well have been written by a man.

An Inquiry into the Duties of the Female Sex by the Revd Thomas Gisborne (1758–1846) was published in 1797. Gisborne, the curate of St James' Church, Barton-under-Needwood in Staffordshire, was a poet and a writer on religious and moral matters.

This religious conduct manual covers a wide range of topics including female education, introducing young women into society, choosing a husband, bringing up children and how women should occupy their free time.

A Father's Legacy to His Daughters by Dr John Gregory (1724–73) was written in 1761. Gregory was a Scottish physician and writer on medical, religious and moral matters.

This letter contains advice on such topics as religion, friendship, relationships with men, courtship and marriage. It was written after the death of the author's wife, to honour her memory and to record her views on female education. The letter was intended only to be given to Gregory's daughters after his death, but it was published by his son in 1774 and became a bestseller.

Essays Addressed to Young Married Women, written by Elizabeth Griffith (1727–93), was published in 1782. Griffith was a dramatist, fiction writer, essayist and actress.

This collection of short essays was written for recently married women and women who were about to marry. The author used her own experience of thirty years of happy marriage when writing the essays. The subjects covered include friendship, temper, neatness, and parental and filial affection.

An Unfortunate Mother's Advice to her Absent Daughters in a Letter to Miss Pennington by Sarah Pennington (1740–83) was published in 1761. Lady Pennington was the estranged wife of Sir Joseph Pennington of Water Hall in Yorkshire. She wrote this book of guidance for her daughters, to whom she was denied access following her separation from their father. She advises them on a number of matters including religion, dress, education, choosing a husband and running a home. This book was widely read and went into three editions in the year following its publication.

A Letter to a Very Young Lady on Her Marriage was written by Jonathan Swift (1667–1745) and published in 1723. Swift, who was Dean of St Patrick's Cathedral in Dublin, was a satirist, essayist, poet and author of political pamphlets. His best known work is *Gulliver's Travels,* published in 1726.

The identity of the young lady to whom the letter is addressed has never been firmly established. Swift was a friend of her parents and her husband. In his letter

Swift advises the recipient on how to conduct herself as a married woman and, most importantly, how to gain and preserve the friendship and esteem of her husband.

A Letter of Genteel and Moral Advice to a Young Lady. In which is digested, into a new and familiar Method, a System of Rules and Informations, to qualify the Fair Sex to be useful and happy in every State by the Reverend Wetenhall Wilkes (1705–51) was published in 1741. Wilkes was at one time the minister of a chapel in Hounslow before becoming the rector of a parish in Lincolnshire. He was also a poet and an author of books on theology, history, and hunting as well as instruction manuals for women. This manual includes advice on courtship, choosing a husband and the duties of a married woman.

Thoughts on the Education of Daughters with Reflections on Female Conduct in the More Important Duties of Life by Mary Wollstonecraft (1759–97) was published in 1787. Wollstonecraft, who was a feminist, writer, philosopher and advocate of women's rights, was the wife of the philosopher William Godwin and the mother of Mary Shelley, the author of *Frankenstein*. Her best known work is *A Vindication of the Rights of Women* (1792).

In this work Wollstonecraft advises on topics such as female accomplishments, moral discipline, love and marriage.

A Fashionable Wedding in St Martin-in-the-Fields Church, London.
From a painting by William Hogarth.

Bibliography

Primary Sources

A Lady, *The Whole Duty of a Woman or a Guide to the Female Sex from the Age of Sixteen to Sixty (1695)*.

Charlotte Dorrington and Freeman, Charles, *The New Lover's Instructor: or, Whole Art of Courtship, Being the Lover's Complete Library and Guide* (c. 1780).

Gisborne, Thomas, *An Enquiry into the Duties of the Female Sex* (1797).

Gregory, John, *A Father's Legacy to His Daughters* (1761).

Griffith, Elizabeth, *Essays Addressed to Young Married Women* (1782).

Pennington, Sarah, *An Unfortunate Mother's Advice to her Absent Daughters, in a Letter to Miss Pennington* (1761).

Swift, Jonathan, *A Letter to a Very Young Lady on her Marriage* (1723).

Wilkes, Wetenhall, *A Letter of Genteel and Moral Advice to a Young Lady. In which is digested, into a new and familiar method, a system of rules and informations, to qualify the Fair Sex to be useful and happy in every state* (1741).

Wollstonecraft, Mary, *Thoughts on the Education of Daughters With Reflections on Female Conduct in the More Important Duties of Life* (1787).

The Family Magazine; A Repository of Religious Instruction and Rational Amusement.

The Gentleman's Magazine.

The Lady's Magazine: or, Entertaining Companion for the Fair Sex.

The Lady's Monthly Museum; or, Polite repository of amusement and instruction: being an assemblage of whatever can tend to please the fancy, interest the mind, or exalt the character of the British fair.

The New Lady's Magazine or Companion for the Fair Sex.

Secondary Sources

Amy, Helen, *Jane Austen* (Amberley Publishing: 2013).

Austen-Leigh, William and Richard Arthur, and Deirdre Le Faye, *Jane Austen, A Family Record* (The British Library: 1989).

Jones, Hazel, *Jane Austen and Marriage* (Continuum: 2009).

Klingel Ray, Joan, *Jane Austen For Dummies* (Wiley Publishing: 2006).

Also available from Amberley Publishing

Jane Austen

HELEN AMY

Available from all good bookshops or to order direct
Please call **01453-847-800**
www.amberley-books.com